# TORTURES OF THE
# TOWER OF LONDON

# TORTURES
## OF THE
# TOWER OF
# LONDON

### G. Abbott

Yeoman Warder (retd)

HM Tower of London
Member of Her Majesty's Bodyguard of the
Yeomen of the Guard Extraordinary

*Verses by*
*Shelagh Abbott*

DAVID & CHARLES
Newton Abbot  London

**British Library Cataloguing in Publication Data**

Abbott, G.
   Tortures of the Tower of London.
   1. Tower of London—History  2. Political
   prisoners—England—London—History
   3. Torture—England—London—History
   I. Title
   364.6'09421'5      HV8599.G7

   ISBN 0–7153–8728–6

Photoset in Bembo by
Northern Phototypesetting Co, Bolton
and printed in Great Britain
by A. Wheaton & Co Ltd, Exeter and London
for David & Charles Publishers plc
Brunel House, Newton Abbot, Devon

# CONTENTS

# Introduction

*'. . . the Queen's servants, the warders of the Tower, whose office it is to put the prisoners to the rack . . .' declaration on behalf of Elizabeth I, 1593.*

Although the Tower of London has been many things during its nine centuries of existence – fortress and royal residence, court and jewel house, mint and zoo – it has always been associated in the public's mind with torture and executions. Despite this reputation, which has been exaggerated in books and films, only a small proportion of the Tower's thousands of prisoners suffered such torments. But the fact that they were tortured at all warrants an account of the instruments used, and the experiences of those who endured them.

The Tower was not, of course, the only place where torture and execution were inflicted: harsh punishments were a way of life in those early centuries. Villages had their stocks and branks, towns their jougs, stangs, and drunkard's cloaks; while many a rural hilltop was crowned by a creaking gibbet. The devices' names were quaint, but the pain they caused was real enough. In order, then, to keep the Tower's record in perspective, it is necessary to include methods of torture and punishment in use throughout the whole country, and to define the difference between the two terms.

Torture, from the Latin *torquere* meaning 'to twist', was not a punishment, but was a forcible persuasion to compel the offender to admit guilt or reveal the names of accomplices. Following such admissions, the trial went ahead and suitable punishment was awarded. The maximum penalty was death – capital punishment from the Latin *caput* meaning 'head' – that is, hanging or decapitation.

Under English common law, torture was illegal, but it could be authorised by the sovereign or the Privy Council. The earliest torture in the Tower is recorded in the fifteenth century during the reign of Henry VI, and the practice was not discontinued until 1640. However, punishments just as painful were still awarded by courts throughout the country which had a wide variety of instruments at their disposal, from the whip to the bridle, the branding iron to the stocks.

Hundreds of minor offences carried the death penalty. Although this punishment had been abolished by William the Conqueror, who replaced it with mutilation and blinding, it was re-introduced by Henry I in 1108. Differing methods of execution were employed throughout the centuries; nooses tightened and blades fell, causing varying degrees of agony to the victims. During the seven or so centuries when execution was a public spectacle it provided a considerable amount of free entertainment for the masses.

Human suffering was not viewed in the same way as it is today, for life was cheap in an age when diseases raged and life expectancy was short. The commonplace sight of bodies hanging in chains, and of skulls and dismembered limbs impaled on city gates, created a callous population who would jeer at a harlot in a ducking stool, pelt a swindler in the stocks, and applaud as a highwayman's legs jerked in the empty air.

So frequent were the tortures and punishments, that in an age when few could write, and records were considered unnecessary, the exact numbers of victims will never be known. But merely to list and describe the instruments used would only be half the story. Extensive research into the Tower's history, through state papers, eye witness reports, and a multitude of other sources has provided the other, human, account of what happened when these vicious implements were actually applied. Visitors to the Tower will be able to glean further historical details from the ever knowledgeable Yeoman Warders on duty there. This body of men, formed in 1078 to guard the castle, its royal residents, and its prisoners, included in its medieval duties assistance in the torturing of prisoners and attendance at the executions of those doomed to die.

Whether such penalties acted as deterrents in those days is a question I leave to others. Even now, in some countries, backs flinch beneath the whip, hands are severed and heads roll. A perusal of the following pages will leave the reader in no doubt in which country and century he – or she – would prefer to live!

# 1 In Durance Vile

*When the tide doth rise*
*The rats shall come*
*And ye shall hear the hell-bent hum*
*Of ravening voices small and thin*
*Chilling thy timid heart within.*
*I can offer no comfort — proffer no cheer,*
*'Twas thine own evil treachery*
*Brought thee here.*

Man's primitive fear of being confined in the darkness has been used through the ages as both torture and punishment, and nowhere more than in castle dungeons. The Tower of London was perfectly suited for this kind of confinement and, although it is not apparent to the casual visitor of today, many traces still remain of secret passages and hidden cells.

These reports have come to us down the ages: 8 February 1581 – Thomas Briscous, Roman Catholic – held in the Pit for five months; 27 March 1581 – Alexander Bryant, priest – loaded with irons and flung into the Pit; November 1577 – Thomas Sherwood – put into 'the dungeon amongst the ratts', later to be racked and hanged; March 1534 – John Bawde, for helping Alice Tankerville to escape from the Tower – put into Little Ease cell in the White Tower – also racked and hanged.

With the passing of time it is difficult to discover exactly where the various 'holes' were located. As towers within the castle were put to other uses, so cellars were filled in and passages bricked up, while subsidence caused many tunnels to collapse. But residing in the Tower of London gives one the opportunity to study the construction of the various buildings and to be present during excavations. Theories can be evolved which, as none of the original plans survive, are worthy of consideration.

Over the centuries the names of the cells were applied to different places of confinement and there could have been many pits or rat infested dungeons. There is a general consensus of opinion, however, that one dark hole, Little Ease, which is now just a broad doorway in the basement of the White Tower, was at one time a stone alcove with a heavy timber door. This would form a cavity about four feet square and nine feet high, making it impossible for the occupant to lie down. There, in the pitch darkness, he could only crouch on the damp earth floor, cold, hungry and miserable, and gradually become disorientated.

Beyond Little Ease is the sub-crypt of St John's Chapel, a gloomy chamber forty-seven feet long and fifteen feet wide. It was originally windowless, and is referred to in old books as 'the Pit'. Fearsome as this vault must have been to a prisoner, rumour has it that below it, under the modern flooring, is a further subterranean cellar which would be a thousand times worse.

Thomas Sherwood and others in the sixteenth century are reported to have been incarcerated in 'the dongeon amongst the ratts' and this could have been a cellar of one of the towers bordering the river, such as the Well Tower. These, however, being on the outer wall, were less escape proof, and it is far more likely that the hole referred to was situated beneath the south-west corner of the White Tower. When, in the last century, the well in that building was discovered, a passageway was also revealed running south towards the river. In recent years, during the construction of the modern History Gallery, another length of passage was uncovered extending in the same direction.

This passage, ending at the river's edge beneath the wharf, could well have admitted the waters at high tide, which would have driven the rats, scampering and squeaking, ahead of it through iron grilles into the cave beneath the White Tower's south-west turret. A hideous fate indeed for the poor wretches imprisoned in its black coldness!

In constructing a castle such as the Tower of London, there was ample scope for incorporating hidden rooms, useful not only as cells but also as refuges or for storing valuables. The twenty small towers and mounts situated along the two encircling walls of the castle were interconnected by the ramparts so that defenders could move rapidly along the battlements as required. These apparently solid walls, eight to twelve feet thick were, in many places, honeycombed with passages and could be entered from the lower levels of the towers. Some of these passages, with side rooms, still survive; others are only evident by bricked up archways and arrow-slits.

Little Ease, the Tower of London

Any large fortress built for a royal household and its garrison of soldiers had to have plenty of storage space for food, arms, and similar supplies in case of siege; and there is little doubt that most of the small towers had deep cellars beneath them, some for use as dungeons when necessary.

One dungeon in the Tower of London was known as 'Little Hell' or 'Lytle Helle', and this is believed to have been the Flint Tower, on the north wall, a tower completely rebuilt in 1796. The next tower, ninety feet to the east, is the Bowyer Tower, now used to house the torture instruments. Beneath its floor is a flight of steps leading down to passageways and underground rooms, all unfortunately filled up with earth many years ago.

On the eastern wall stands the Broad Arrow Tower, little restored or modernised, and its walls bear many inscriptions carved by sixteenth-century prisoners: John Daniell 1556, hanged on Tower Hill for treason, Thomas Forde 1582, a priest executed in Elizabeth's reign, and many others. In recent years explorations revealed a deep cellar beneath the tower, a vault blocked up with rubble which yielded shards of ancient pottery and scores of eighteenth-century bottles and containers. Other towers, the Salt and the Beauchamp in particular, had lower rooms half underground, all of them fitting places for those reluctant to confess. Prisoners loaded with irons and thrust into impenetrable darkness did not prove stubborn for long.

## How do you plead?

When on trial, it was necessary for the accused person to plead guilty or not guilty to the charges brought against him. But the old laws stated that, if found guilty of a capital offence, the prisoner would not only lose his life, but also forfeit his lands and property to the State leaving his family destitute. If, however, he deliberately refused to plead, he was subjected to agonising 'persuasion' which could result in death. And since his death would therefore occur before trial and verdict, the State would have no claim on his lands, and his family could then inherit them.

Some prisoners took advantage of this and refused to plead, not wanting their conviction and execution to stain their family honour. They were then adjudged 'mute of malice' – wilfully silent – and were warned of the dire consequences should they persist in their refusal to plead.

The earliest method of persuasion, dating from 1275, was that of *prison forte et dure* which meant strong and severe imprisonment or, more simply, starvation. Chained in a cold dank cell, the prisoner was given bad bread with no water one day; then dirty water – with no bread – the next day. Because slow starvation was a lingering death, most prisoners eventually gave in and pleaded either guilty or not guilty. One woman who didn't give in was Cecilia de Rygeway who was accused in 1357 of murdering her husband. Staying mute, she was subjected to *prison forte et dure* but survived without adequate food and drink for over forty days. This so impressed King Edward III that he pardoned her.

Starvation was always a useful measure to apply to prisoners. In the Tower, a Jesuit priest Alexander Briant ate the clay from his prison walls rather than submit, though later, on 1 December 1581, he was hanged, disembowelled and quartered at Tyburn. Even ordinary debtors were denied sustenance in some prisons. Until their debts

The *peine forte et dure*, 1721

were paid, prisoners housed in Winchester's city gates had to survive by 'fishing' through holes in the floor for food parcels attached to the lines by sympathetic passers-by.

As a method of persuasion starvation was harsh, but in 1405 it was greatly increased in severity by the introduction of a new penalty, *peine forte et dure*. The prisoner was given barley bread on one day, puddle water the next, as before, but there the similarity ended. The treatment can best be summed up by an extract from the Newgate Prison records of January 1720, in respect of two highwaymen, William Spiggot and Thomas Phillips. As they refused to plead, the court directed:

> that the prisoner be put in a mean room, stopped from the light, and there be laid on the bare ground, without any litter, straw or other covering, and without any garment about him except a cloth about his middle. He shall lie on his back, his head shall be covered, and his feet shall be bare. One of his arms shall be drawn with a cord to one side of the room and the other arm to the other side; and his legs shall be served in the like manner. Then there shall be laid upon his body as much iron or stone as he can bear, and more. And the first day after, he shall have three morsels of barley bread without any drink, and the second day he shall be allowed to drink as much as he can, at three times, of the water that is nearest the prison door, except running water, without any bread. And this shall be his diet till he pleads or dies.

On hearing this, Phillips immediately changed his mind. Stubborn Spiggot, however, was spreadeagled and, despite breaking his bonds several times, was finally secured and subjected to a weight of 350lb. After half an hour, the addition of a further 50lb on his body had the desired effect, forcing him to plead. For two days he could hardly speak and, on regaining his speech, described how he went into a numbed coma under the appalling pressure. Both men pleaded not guilty and both were convicted and subsequently hanged at Tyburn.

One of the many who died in the Press Yard or Press Room of their prisons was Major George Strangeways, who in 1659 refused to plead to the murder of his brother-in-law. He submitted to the press and so extreme was the pain that he begged the onlookers to add their weight to the iron already there. Out of mercy they obliged, standing on the board placed on him, and he died within ten minutes.

One not so determined as the Major was Nathaniel Hawes, accused of robbery in 1721. After only seven minutes beneath a weight of

250lb, he begged for release and was later convicted and hanged, as was another robber named Barnworth, alias Frasier, who is reputed to have borne an incredible 450lb when imprisoned at Kingston, Surrey in 1726.

Although *peine forte et dure* was not classed as torture but as a legal persuasion, it was illegal to use it as capital punishment – to actually sentence a person to be pressed to death. Nevertheless, this sentence was occasionally delivered, the last time being in Ireland in 1740. Matthew Ryan, caught robbing on the highway, feigned lunacy and then dumbness in court, in order to avoid pleading. The jury agreed that he was acting wilfully, and he was given time to consider the awful consequences. On being returned to court, he persisted in his silence and was sentenced to be pressed to death in public. He was carried to the market place in Kilkenny and there secured. No record survives of the weight he bore and, despite his pleas to be hanged, weights were added until the court's sentence had been satisfied.

Juries are not infallible of course. At Nottingham in 1735, a deaf mute was pressed to death, the officials, doubtless, marvelling at his resistance. But despite the agonies these prisoners had to suffer, they could be considered fortunate not to have endured a refinement introduced in the reign of Elizabeth I. This increased the severity of the method by placing a stone beneath the victim's back, ultimately breaking his spine.

Nor should it be thought that only men were subjected to such torments. A tragic instance ocurred at York in March 1586 when Margaret Clitheroe was on trial for sheltering a Roman Catholic priest. She refused to plead, and was taken to the Press Room, where, as described in Lingard's *History of England*:

After she had prayed, one of the sheriffs commanded them to put off her apparel, when she, with the four women, requested him on their knees that for the honour of womanhood this might be dispensed with, but they would not grant it. Then she requested that the women might unparrel her, and that they would turn their faces from her during that time. The women took off her clothes and put on her the long linen habit. Then very quietly she laied her down upon the ground, her face covered with a kerchief and most of her body with the habit. The dore was laied upon her, her hands she joined upon her face.

Then the sheriff said 'Naie, ye must have your hands bound'. Two sergeants parted her hands and bound them to two posts in the same manner as the feet had been previously fixed. After this they laied weight upon her which, when she first felt, she said 'Jesu, Jesu, Jesu, have mercye upon mee', which were the last words she was heard to speak.

She was in dying about one quarter of an hower. A sharp stone as big as a man's fist had been put under her back. Upon her was laied the quantity of 800 to 900lb which, breaking her ribs, caused them to burst forth of the skinne.

Sometimes an alternative method was employed to encourage prisoners to plead whereby their thumbs were tied together and the whipcord then twisted. The official performing this task was usually the public executioner and, should he fail to bring a favourable response, the prisoner was then conducted to the press room for *peine forte et dure*. Some of the prisoners previously mentioned were subjected to the twin torments, Phillips, Spiggot and Hawes all had their thumbs constricted tightly before they were put to the press.

The Newgate Sessions of 1663 report the case of George Thorely, who:

... being indicted for robbery, refused to plead, and his two Thumbs were tyed together with Whipcord, that the pain of that might compel him to Plead, and he was sent away so tyed, and a minister with him to perswade him. And an Hour after, he was brought back again, and he pleaded.

Women too, suffered similarly. Mary Andrews, obstinate to the last, endured such violent tightening around her thumbs that three whipcords snapped. The fourth cord, however, proved unbearable and she submitted her plea at her trial in 1721.

Shortly afterwards, society recoiled from applying such barbaric measures to those who would not yield. In 1772 an act was passed whereby those remaining mute would automatically be assumed guilty. Five years later, a murderer, Francis Mercer, refused to plead and the jury came to the conclusion that he was mute, wilfully and not by act of God. No trial was held, and the judge immediately sentenced him to death, his body being dissected afterwards for medical research.

Other cases followed and, with the realisation by more humane lawmakers that all defendants should be deemed innocent until proved guilty by the State, it was finally decreed in 1827 that a refusal to plead would be entered in the trial proceedings as one of 'not guilty'.

# 2 Two Loving Daughters

*'Tis something to lie on a country day*
*Away from the city amid the hay,*
*But another to hark to the cogs' great clack*
*As they inch by inch do lengthen thy back.*
*Speak then, my friend – utter thy plead*
*'Ere thy body breaketh and inward bleed.*

So thick were the walls of the Tower of London, so deep its moat and well-guarded its gates, that almost from the start it was used not only to house royalty but also to imprison enemies of the king and country. Most of its twenty towers, at one time or another, confined prisoners who ranged from Jesuit priests to gunpowder plotters; rebellious lords to female heretics. All of them knew more than they were prepared to divulge, and those who proved stubborn were tortured.

There was a wide range of devices at the authorities' disposal, some more portable than others, and these were taken to the prisoners' cells and applied therein. It is generally recognised, however, that much of the torture took place in the underground chambers of the White Tower, the immense citadel at the very heart of the castle.

A visit to that basement now reveals modern fittings and white walls, daylight streaming in through high windows to illuminate the ordnance and weapons meticulously displayed. But imagine the chamber as it was originally, without doors or windows; take away the museum showpieces and replace the electric lights with a few flickering torches in wall brackets. Realise, as you will, that now the only entrance is down the steep stone spiral stair from the heavily guarded upper floors, just as it was for centuries. And listen to the Jesuit Father John Gerard, who said:

> We went to the torture room in a kind of solemn procession, the guards walking ahead with lighted candles. The chamber was

Torture chamber, the Tower of London

underground and dark, particularly near the entrance. It was a vast, shadowy place and every device and instrument of human torture was there. They pointed out some of them to me and said I should have to taste them. Then they asked me again if I would confess. 'I cannot' I said.

That the torture was intensive is evidenced by the report of the Secretary of State, Winwood, when interrogating Edward Peacham in the Tower in 1614. 'Peacham was this day examined before torture, in torture, between torture and after torture; yet he persists in his insensible denials.'

The torture most feared was the rack, and until comparatively recent times, holes in the vault's floor were reputed to have been the sockets for the legs of this device. The instrument was introduced into the Tower from the continent in 1420 by John Holland, Duke of Exeter, when he was Constable of the Tower and so, with the macabre humour of the times, victims secured to the rack were said to be 'wedded to the Duke of Exeter's Daughter', doubtless a wife they could hardly wait to divorce!

As well as being Constable, the Duke led an adventurous life, fighting valiantly against the French at Agincourt, Caen and Rouen. Now his remains, together with those of two of his wives, lie in a magnificent chantry tomb within the Chapel Royal of St Peter ad Vincula, only yards from where so many had suffered on the device he had brought to the Tower.

The machine itself, modified and 'improved' during its lifetime, was an open rectangular frame of oak, over six feet long, which was raised three feet from the floor on four legs. The prisoner was laid beneath it on his back, and his wrists and ankles were attached by ropes to a windlass or axle at each end of the frame. These were operated by levers turned in opposite directions, hoisting the victim off the floor until level with the frame, his weight tending to dislocate his joints at shoulders and hips, elbows and knees. The ropes were held taut by ratchets on the windlasses so that the pain could be sustained while questions were asked. Further leverage was applied to overcome continued resistance.

The official rackmaster in Tudor times was Thomas Norton, who boasted that he had stretched the Jesuit martyr Alexander Briant 'a foot longer than God had made him'. His assistants in the torture chamber were the yeoman warders (see *The Beefeaters of the Tower of London*, David & Charles, 1985), and when, in Elizabeth's reign, it was said that the rack seldom stood idle in the Tower, her minister Burghley sought to allay public concern by issuing a report recorded in the state papers of 1583:

Torture by the rack in the Tower of London

The Queen's servants, the warders, whose office and act it is to handle the rack, were ever by those that attended the examinations, specially charged to use it in as charitable manner as such a thing might be.

However, it is impossible to inflict pain painlessly!

The warders' superior officer, the Lieutenant of the Tower, usually received precise instructions. In the council books for 15 March 1559, Sir Richard Blount was ordered to interrogate two men, Pitt and Nicholls, who if they proved obstinate were 'to be brought to the rack, and to feel the smart there if as the examinees by their discretion shall think good, for the better boulting out of the truth of the matter.'

Many others found out just how painful the rack could be. Perhaps the best known case is that of Guy (or Guido) Fawkes, who was one of a large group of Catholic extremists seeking in 1605 to overthrow James I and his government by blowing up the royal family and Parliament. After an anonymous letter had been received by Lord Monteagle, warning him not to attend Parliament that day, a search trapped Fawkes in the very act of preparing the barrels of gunpowder stacked in the cellars beneath. In the Council Chamber of the Lieutenant's Lodgings (now known as the Queen's House) Guy Fawkes was closely questioned. Fanatical and stubborn, he resisted, and was threatened with sterner measures. The King himself had written that 'if he will not other wayes confesse, the gentler tortours are to be first used unto him *et sic per gradus ad ima tenditur*, and so god spede youre goode worke.'

And 'spede' it they did, taking Fawkes to the torture chamber in the White Tower. As was customary, he was first shown the devices ranged around the room, the very sight of which proved sufficient with some prisoners; but Fawkes was made of sterner stuff. He was therefore secured to the rack and its levers were turned. Over him leant the questioners, the Secretary of State, the Lord Privy Seal and the Lord High Admiral; for this was the King's business and not to be delegated. No sound escaped through the fifteen foot thick walls to the outside world as the ropes creaked, the ratchets clicked and the incessant questions urged and probed.

For thirty minutes — although it must have seemed an aeon of agony to the tormented wretch on the frame, the interrogators' questions went unanswered. Then Fawkes gasped his surrender; he divulged a few vital facts, then hesitated. Once again the levers were pushed, straining the ropes even tighter around the axles, stretching Fawkes' sinews to snapping point, forcing his hip and shoulder joints from their sockets. And then, 'when told he must come to it againe and againe, from daye to daye, till he should have delivered his whole knowledge', he confessed.

Names, dates and meeting places spilled forth, damning and incriminating his fellow conspirators with every whispered word written down by his inquisitors. Later, with a hand literally racked in pain, he could only scrawl his name to his confession, the document which would be in effect the death certificate of so many. Together with seven of his fellow plotters, namely Bates, Grant, Rookewood, Digby, Keys, and the two Wintour brothers, he was hanged, disembowelled whilst still alive, and quartered.

Three Jesuit priests, Fathers Oldcorne, Garnet, and Gerard were believed to be implicated. Oldcorne and Garnet were arrested and incarcerated in the Bloody Tower. Gerard was taken to the Salt Tower from where he later made a daring escape. Father Henry Garnet was racked no fewer than twenty-five times it is reported, and on 3 May 1606, he was dragged to St Paul's Cathedral, in front of which he was hanged and quartered. Edward Oldcorne was stretched five times on the rack, and was hanged, disembowelled and quartered at Worcester.

Very different was the case of Sir Thomas Wyatt, friend and admirer of Anne Boleyn and her daughter Elizabeth. In 1554 he raised a revolt against the accession of Mary to the throne, and marched to London. Wyatt bombarded the Tower from across the river doing little damage but, firing on the lieutenant's barge, killed the boatman – though the passenger, a Tower warder, escaped uninjured. He then attacked Westminster, only to have his small army of two thousand Kentishmen defeated, and at 5 pm on 8 February he was brought, captive, through Traitors' Gate and imprisoned in the Bell Tower.

The authorities, suspecting a conspiracy to remove Mary and place Princess Elizabeth on the throne, wasted no time. Wyatt was racked repeatedly and then condemned to death as a rebel. On the Tower Hill scaffold he denied any involvement with Elizabeth, and died a traitor's death, being hanged and quartered. His head was fixed on a spike in Mayfair, and parts of his dismembered body were exhibited on the city gates.

In Tudor times sexual discrimination hardly existed, at least not where the rack was concerned. It didn't matter whether wrists and ankles were slim and feminine, or sinewy and masculine; questions were there to be answered, and the rack was there to persuade and encourage. When Catherine Parr, last wife of Henry VIII, was suspected by her enemies at Court of having Protestant inclinations, her companions were taken into custody; for if the queen could be incriminated, a third royal head might well roll on Tower Green.

Anne Askew, a close friend of Catherine Parr's, was a highly intelligent and fervent reformer who had sought to convert the queen to her own Protestant beliefs. She was arrested, tried, and condemned to death by burning – the usual fate of heretics. After her trial she was taken to the Tower to be questioned further about the queen's involvement by the Lord Chancellor Sir Thomas Wriothesley, Sir Richard Rich, and the Tower's Lieutenant, Sir Anthony Knivett. She would volunteer no information and so, in order to terrify her, she was taken to the White Tower dungeon and shown the instruments of torture. She refused to be frightened so easily, and the chancellor then ordered the lieutenant's warders to rack her.

She was tied in position and the levers were slowly operated: the questions came, but no answers. Anne Askew, a strong willed martyr, was determined to tell them nothing. The chancellor, equally determined, ordered more pressure on the levers, more agony for the victim, his orders being endorsed by Sir Richard Rich who, eleven years earlier, had perjured himself in order to bring about the execution of Sir Thomas More.

The lieutenant was appalled by their brutality and ordered his men to release her, whereupon Wriothesley and Rich seized the levers themselves and, according to Anne's own testimony quoted in *Foxe's Book of Martyrs*:

> They did put me on the rack because I confessed no ladies or gentlemen to be of my opinion, and thereupon kept me a long time on it and because I lay still and did not cry out, My Lord Chancellor and Master Rich took pains to rack me with their own hands, till I was nigh dead.

And, as summed up by the historian Bale, 'So quietly and patiently praying to the Lord, she endured their tyranny till her bones and joints were almost plucked asunder.' At the sight of her suffering, the lieutenant stated his intention to appeal direct to the King, a right which exists to this day. The chancellor, not to be outmanoeuvred, left the Tower on horseback and headed for Westminster and the royal presence, unaware that the lieutenant's barge lay moored and ready at Tower Wharf. The tide was favourable, and the fast flowing river was always speedier than the muddy cobbled streets! First to the King, the lieutenant's account was accepted. The torture was halted, and the fainting, half-crippled woman was revived by the Tower's surgeon. She was, however, still a heretic; and so later, in 1546, she was carried, strapped to a chair, to Smithfield where she was publicly burned at the stake.

The application of torture for any reason was finally declared illegal by royal commission in 1628, although cases did still occur for a further twelve years. The commission was set up as the result of the trial of a murderer, John Felton, lieutenant in a company of foot. In August 1628 Felton, a stout swarthy man, bought a sheath knife in a shop on Tower Hill, a weapon described by the historian Carlisle as 'of value thirteen pence, of short broad blade with sharp trowel point.' Felton then went to Portsmouth where troops were mobilising for France and, seizing his opportunity, fatally stabbed their commander, George Villiers, Duke of Buckingham.

Felton was immediately arrested and taken to the Tower of London. There, in the Bloody Tower, he was interrogated by the Earl of Dorset and William Laud, Bishop of London. When Felton denied having accomplices, his inquisitors threatened him with the rack. It was then that Felton uttered one remark, a statement so obvious that it is hard to understand why it had never been made before – he simply stated that torture was illegal, adding daringly, 'If I be put upon the rack I will accuse you, my Lord Dorset, and none but yourself.' (State Papers).

Thus challenged, the bishop referred the matter to Charles I, who delegated the decision to the royal commission mentioned above. Their findings were, as recorded in *State Trials* vol iii, 'Felton ought not by the law to be tortured by the rack, for no such punishment is known or allowed by our law.' Not that it really helped Felton. Although he had thus sidestepped the rack, no similarly inspired remark helped him to escape the gallows at Tyburn where, on 29 November 1628, he was hanged. His body was taken by coach to the scene of his crime, where it was suspended in chains from a gibbet. The diarist John Evelyn witnessed it, and wrote 'His dead body is carried down to Portsmouth, and hangs there high; I hear it creak in the wind.'

Despite the commission's decision, the Tower's rack still appeared in the inventory of stores for 1678, being shown as the 'Rack for Torment'. It was destroyed, together with thousands of weapons and much militaria, when the Great Storehouse opposite the White Tower was burnt down in 1841.

The last time it was actually used was in 1640 and, by a strange coincidence, William Laud, by then Archbishop of Canterbury, was again involved. During rioting in the City in May, the archbishop's residence, Lambeth Palace, was attacked. One of those arrested was John Archer, a young man who had been at the front of the mob leading them by beating a drum. Sir William Balfour, Lieutenant of the Tower, was instructed to show him the rack and, if he failed to name his accomplices, he was to be racked 'as in your and the examiners discretions shall be thought fit' (Tower Records). These orders were of course obeyed, and John Archer's small claim to fame, one which, doubtless, he would gladly have declined given the chance, is that of being the last person recorded as having been racked. His ultimate fate is unknown.

The coincidence involving Archbishop Laud stretched almost as remorselessly as the rack itself, for the man who threatened Felton with the rack in the Bloody Tower, and whose damaged palace led to Archer being racked, was himself accused of treason and sent to the Tower of London in 1641. Fittingly, he too was imprisoned in the Bloody Tower and, four years later, in January 1645 at the age of 71, William Laud, Archbishop of Canterbury, was beheaded by the axe on the public execution site on Tower Hill.

It should not be thought, however, that the Tower rack was the only one in the country. In fact, there was one actually installed and in use in a private house. During the persecution of the Jesuits in the sixteenth century, many priests were hunted down and interrogated by Richard Topcliffe, who had been authorised by the government 'to torment priests in his own house in such a manner as he shall think good.' This hated and feared persecutor boasted that the rack in the Tower was child's play compared with his.

As a Member of Parliament he had recruited a team countrywide, whose task was to pursue and capture fugitive priests. Rewards were paid for each arrest, in addition to travelling expenses of thirteen pence per mile levied from the victims. For this lucrative income the bounty hunters eavesdropped in taverns, spied on Catholic families and searched suspected houses, tearing down walls and partitions in their hunt for hidden priest holes. After arrest, the priests were taken to London and delivered to Topcliffe who racked them unmercifully in his private torture chamber. He and his band of official priest catchers were responsible for the deaths of scores of Roman Catholics, many of whom were burned at the stake.

Another rack was in use in Ireland and in 1628 some criminals were tortured to compel them to testify against the Byrne family of Wicklow, thought to be conspiring against Charles I. The 'witnesses' were threatened with hanging, and some were put in irons. Two suffered even more; one was racked in Dublin, and the other was put naked on a burning gridiron.

The Tower of London not only had its 'Duke of Exeter's Daughter', it also had 'The Scavenger's Daughter' or, more correctly, 'Skeffington's Daughter' or 'Skeffington's Gyves', named after its inventor Sir Leonard Skeffington. In 1534 Skeffington became Lieutenant of the Tower and, after having studied the rack, proceeded to devise a machine which had precisely the opposite result. Instead of stretching its victims, his machine compressed them or, as described by Matthew Tanner, a Jesuit historian:

> . . . for while the rack drags apart the joints by the feet and hands tied, this one constricts and binds as into a ball. This holds the body in a threefold manner, the lower legs being pressed to the thighs, the thighs to the belly, and thus both are locked with two iron clamps which are pressed by the tormentor's force against each other; the body of the victim is almost broken by this compression. By the cruel torture more dreadful and more complete than the rack, by the cruelty of which the whole body is so bent that with some the blood exudes from the tips of the hands and feet; with others the box of the chest being burst, a quantity of blood is expelled from the mouth and nostrils.

'The Scavenger's Daughter', in the Tower of London, 1580

Various patterns of the device were used. The one now surviving in the Tower consists of an arrangement of iron rods and shackles which, when secured to the doubled up victim and tightened, could well have brought about the results described by Tanner. Another version was an iron hoop with two hinged halves. The victim, doubled up in a kneeling position over one half of the hoop, was then knelt on by his tormentors until the other half could be forced over his back and locked. A screw mechanism tightened the hoop further, the victim having to endure the torture for an hour and a half.

The advantage of Skeffington's Daughter lay in its portability. If necessary, the engine of torment could be moved with comparative ease along winding passages and up narrow spiral stairways for use in other rooms and towers. Most of the time, however, it was kept in the White Tower with the other implements in order to strike terror into those who were shown it. Many of its victims were Jesuit priests such as Robert Nutter who, in February 1584, twice suffered being pinioned in the machine. Two others were Luke Kirby and Thomas Cottam. Brought to the Tower on 5 December 1580, they endured torture in Skeffington's Daughter and, after months of imprisonment, both were finally hanged, disembowelled and quartered at Tyburn on 30 May 1582.

A cell wall within the Beauchamp Tower bears a verse inscribed by Thomas Myagh in which he complains of his 'torture straunge'. Myagh was an Irishman who was believed to have been conspiring with rebels in that country, and therefore in possession of vital information. The Tower bills, the accounts of the lieutenant, for 10 March 1581, state that they had questioned him twice but had not put him in Skeffington's Gyves because they had been ordered to examine him in secrecy 'which they could not do, because that manner of dealing with him required the presence and aid of one of the warders all the time that he would be in those irons', and also because they 'found the man so resolute as in their opinions little would be wrung out of him but by some sharper torture.'

Myagh was interrogated again and, although this time his resolution was severely tested, he divulged nothing as the Tower bill reported a week later – 'notwithstanding that they had made trial of him by the torture of Skeffington's Gyves, and with so much sharpness, as was in their judgement for the man and his cause, enough.'

There was now only one alternative for the authorities, and on 30 July 1581 an instruction was issued to the lieutenant and to rackmaster Norton 'to deal with him with the rack in such sort as they should see fit.' History does not reveal the consequences but without doubt Thomas Myagh never forgot his hours in the embrace of the two loving daughters of the Tower.

A version of the Scavenger's Daughter seems to have existed in Scotland, for in 1596 the Caschielawis, variously known as Cashilaws or Casicaws, was invented by the Master of Orkney. While some accounts describe it as drawing body and limbs forcibly together, others call it an iron frame designed to hold a limb immoveable over a brazier of glowing coals.

# 3 Brakes, Boots, Barnacles, Collars and Cuffs

*When next ye put thy shoes upon*
*Recall that many an Englishman*
*And many a foreigner for that matter*
*Hath hearkened with dread to the torturer's clatter*
*As the Boots, the cursèd Boots were used*
*Till with legs as matchwood he screamed bemused.*

Little is known about the torture instrument called the brakes and, although it was used in the Tower of London in Tudor times, no specimen has survived. Its design might well have resembled a bridle, for it is described as a device to force out, or break, the victim's teeth. This would be done one tooth at a time, with an incriminating question being put prior to each operation of the machine.

One instance of its reported use occurred when rumours reached Henry VIII concerning scandalous behaviour involving his new queen Catherine Howard and two of his courtiers – Francis Dereham, the queen's cousin, and Thomas Culpepper, Clerk of the Armoury and Gentleman of the King's Chamber. Confessions had to be obtained, and so, in December 1541, a third suspect, Damport, was brought to the Tower and subjected to having his teeth forced out in the brakes. Doubtless this was sufficient to persuade him to turn king's evidence for he was later released.

Dereham and Culpepper both paid the price. After an elaborate trial, they were taken to Tyburn. Dereham, being just a commoner, was publicly hanged, disembowelled while still alive, and quartered. Culpepper, as a Gentleman of the Privy Chamber, had the privilege of being decapitated by the axe. Their heads were displayed on London Bridge, clearly visible to Queen Catherine as she passed beneath them six weeks later en route to Traitors' Gate and her own execution on Tower Green.

A variation of the brakes could well have been used in the thirteenth century on a Bristol man who tried to defraud King John. When he protested that he was unable to pay the fine of £6,500 levied against him, he was ordered to have a tooth forcibly removed each day until the fine was paid. A week was enough to ensure his compliance.

The kings who followed Henry VIII were closely involved with an instrument of torture known as 'the boots', though it was also called 'the brodequins' or 'bootikins'. England did not have a monopoly on torture instruments however, and the boots were imported from France and were widely used in Scotland during the sixteenth and seventeenth centuries. As its name implies, the boots tortured the victim's legs and feet, although there were several varieties of the basic instrument.

The most commonly used method required the victim to be secured in a chair. An upright board was then placed each side of each of his legs, splinting them from knee to ankle, the boards being tied together within a frame, by ropes and iron rings. With the legs now immoveable, wooden wedges were hammered between the inner two boards and then between the outer boards and their surrounding frame, compressing and crushing the trapped legs. An alternative method dispensed with the frame; the seated victim had a board tied each side of each leg bound tightly together. For the 'ordinary' torture, four wedges were driven between the inner two boards. For the 'extraordinary' torture eight wedges were used, bursting flesh and bone and mangling the limbs permanently.

Other variations included iron boots which were put on the victim's feet and then heated. An Irish priest, John Hurley, suffered this treatment in 1583. Elizabeth's Secretary of State, Walsingham, suggested that Hurley's feet 'be toasted at the fire with hot boots'. They duly were, and Hurley was later hanged for treason. Iron boots were also employed in the torture known as the Spanish boots, which crushed the legs by means of a screw mechanism. Another version tightly encased the victim's legs in leggings of damp parchment. So extreme was the shrinkage of this material when the victim was held near the fire, that excruciating agony resulted as the tissues of the legs were compressed.

The Scottish boots, using wedges, were applied to political prisoners, one of whom was William Holt in 1583. Even as late as 1690, Henry Neville Payne, a plotter in a conspiracy against William III, was tortured in the boots and also by the thumbscrews. Two Stuart kings, James I and James II, took an active interest in the boots torture, revealing a lack of pity for the suffering of others. James I frequently visited his royal zoo at the Tower of London, and ordered fights to the death between lions and dogs, bear baiting, and other similar cruelties for his entertainment.

Before his accession to the English throne, when just James VI of Scotland, he was faced with a conspiracy to overthrow him led by the Pretender, Francis, Earl of Bothwell, a notorious dabbler in the black arts and witchcraft. Bothwell's secretary was Dr John Fiennes, a schoolmaster from Saltpans who, like his master, indulged in the casting of spells. In 1591 he and others were accused of raising a storm at sea with the intention of wrecking the ship taking James on a royal visit to Denmark.

Fiennes was given a taste of torture, being racked and then put in the boots. Delirious, he confessed, but on regaining consciousness later, retracted his statement. This time no mercy was shown and King James suggested a new device:

> His nailes upon all his fingers were to be riven and pulled off with an instrument called in Scottish a turkas, which in England is known as a payre of pincers, and under everie nayle there was to be thrust in two needels over, even up to the head.

Crippled, racked, and mutilated, Fiennes resisted to the end, which came at the stake on Castle Hill, Edinburgh where he was burned alive before a vast crowd.

The Scots frequently used the boot torture in cases of witchcraft in the sixteenth century, on women as well as men. In the Orkneys, Thomas Papley and Alison Balfour were both put on trial for practising black magic rituals, and endured the appalling constriction of the Scottish boots.

In the next century James II showed a similar disregard for human suffering. Whilst still Duke of York and High Commissioner for Scotland in 1680, he was fiercely opposed by Archibald Campbell, Earl of Argyll. One of Argyll's servants, a man named Spence, was arrested and closely questioned by Lord Perth and members of the Scots Privy Council. The prisoner was so reluctant to incriminate his master that he was threatened with the customary torture, and it says much for some members of the council that the mere spectacle of the wedges being driven in, filled them with revulsion.

Not all the members recoiled in horror, however, as related by Bishop Burnet in his *History of his Own Time*:

When any are to be stuck in the boots, it is done in the presence of the Council, and upon that happening, almost all offer to run away. The sight is so dreadful that without an order restraining such a number to stay, the boards would remain unused. But the Duke of York, while he was in Scotland, was so far from running away that he looked on all the while with an unmoved indifference, and with an attention as if he were watching a curious experiment. This gave a terrible impression of him to all that observed it, as a man that had no bowels of humanity in him.

Evidently sufficient members of the council were induced to stay as witnesses and inquisitors, for Spence was subjected to the boots, enduring the splintering agony as the mallet drove the wedges deeper between the boards. Somehow he found the will to resist, so further measures were applied. He was deprived of sleep for more than a week, and was then put to the torment of the thumbscrews, a device which finally forced him to yield. His ultimate fate is unknown, but his master, the Earl of Argyll, was subsequently charged with treason. Although he escaped to England and later to Holland, the Earl was caught in June 1685 and executed by the Scottish Maiden, an implement of justice described in chapter 8.

Of the last item of this type, 'the barnacles', little is known. It has been said to resemble a short rod with a loop of cord at one end. The victim's upper lip was pulled through the loop, which was then tightened. Subsequent twisting of the rod resulted in acute pain and eventual mutilation. Its use was probably limited, as its operation would prevent the victim from confessing, or indeed, saying anything at all.

## Collars and cuffs

Although this book was not intended to include devices designed solely for restraint, such as handcuffs and leg irons, some devices had a dual role of both restraint and torture. As such they deserve mention, especially those which were employed in the Tower.

In the inventory for 1547 the entry 'stele collar for a prysonr' appears, and it is probably the same one now exhibited in the Tower. More generally known as the iron collar or Spanish collar, it is designed to be locked tightly around the victim's neck, and would be worn for weeks if not months. The initial discomfort of wearing it would soon be replaced by actual pain, for the inside is lined with short, sharp studs. At one time the collar was filled with lead for extra weight, but even without that ballast it weighs ten pounds. Worn night and day, the collar would quickly sap the victim's resistance and deter any attempts to escape. Such devices were used in many prisons in the eighteenth century to confine highwaymen and incorrigible rogues.

A very similar device was the jougs, widely used in Scotland from the sixteenth to the eighteenth centuries. The jougs, also known as 'the bregan' or the bradyeans, was rather less harsh than the iron collar. It lacked the sharp studs and the extra weight, being just a narrow metal collar attached by a chain to the market cross, prison gate, or church doorway therefore inflicting public shame rather than actual pain. Those committing minor crimes or offending the church were put in the jougs, the hinged ring being locked about their necks while the townsfolk gathered to jeer and abuse.

In 1574 David Leyes, having struck his father, was sentenced to two hours in the jougs and afterwards paraded through the town whilst in Dumfries, Bessie Black, having been found lacking in virtue, had to stand in the jougs at the market cross on six Sabbaths for all to see.

Not all such penances ended harmlessly however. In 1541 John Porter was arrested for the crime of reading the Bible, and was taken to Newgate Prison. He was left in the jougs for several days and subsequently found dead – apparently he had fainted and been strangled by the collar.

As the collar and the jougs gripped the victim's neck, the bilboes gripped the ankles. This device consisted of a long iron bar, one end of which was secured to the floor. Free to slide along the bar were hinged iron rings, which were riveted about the ankles of the prisoners forcing them to sit or lie down for weeks on end. The one displayed in the Tower, having only two rings, was designed for just one prisoner, but longer ones could obviously accommodate more.

The name is a corruption of the Spanish town Bilbao for, when the Armada was defeated in 1588, chests of these shackles were found in the galleons, reputedly to pinion English captives. In actual fact, similar devices were widely used for naval prisoners on board ship, and the Royal Navy was equipped with them until the eighteenth century. English prisons also found them invaluable for restricting inmates while they were being flogged, and the punishment cell in Newgate Prison was given the name Bilboe or Bilbow.

In the state prison of the Tower of London two categories of captivity existed for those who were held there. The well behaved ones were given the 'liberty of the leads', permitting them to walk the battlements for air and exercise. Their troublesome counterparts

were 'close confined', restricted under guard in their prison rooms
and secured by wrist and ankle with chains. These chains were given
various names, but generally leg irons were known as fetters.
Manacles encircled wrists, and shackles secured fetters to manacles.
When these were worn for long periods, flesh would become raw
and lacerated and every movement would be agonising. Leg irons
weighed as much as 14lb, and were riveted on by the Tower
blacksmith.

In February 1584 a priest, Robert Nutter, was not only fettered in
the Tower for forty-three days, but, as already mentioned, suffered
two embraces of the Scavenger's Daughter. Another martyr,
Nicholas Horner, was fettered so tightly that 'one of his legs rotted
and had to be cut off in the Justice Hall.'

Many castles and prisons used these devices, and particularly fine
specimens are on display at Lancaster Castle as well as at the Tower.
The more dangerous the criminal, the greater the weight of his 'sute
of yrons'. On Tuesday 3 January 1693, James Whitney, ringleader of
a gang of eighty highwaymen, was finally captured. Close confined
in Newgate Prison, he was immobilised by 40lb of iron attached to
his legs, and was hanged a month later. Some leg irons were joined by
heavy links of such length that it was only with extreme difficulty
that the prisoner could move at all. Yet determined men would
always persevere.

The notorious housebreaker and felon Jack Sheppard, hero of
many escapes and idol of the public, was finally locked up in 'the
castle', the name given to a strongroom in Newgate. Although
handcuffed, loaded with long leg irons and chained to a staple fixed
in the floor, his dexterity with a small nail unlocked his bonds and he
got away again, breaking through walls and scaling the prison roof.
Alas for him, on 16 November 1724, Tyburn tree claimed him and he
swung from the gallows, pitied by the mob and lamented by
London's underworld.

Women too felt the cruel grip of fetters about their ankles. Mary
Blandy, accused of poisoning her father, was suspected of planning to
escape from custody and put in irons. Later these were changed for
heavier fetters and these were not removed until her trial. She was
found guilty and sentenced to death. At 9am on 6 April 1752, wearing
black bombazine and with her wrists bound with black ribbon, she
mounted the first few steps of the ladder positioned beneath the
gallows. Pausing, she exclaimed, 'Gentlemen, don't hang me high,
for the sake of decency.' She mounted two more steps and then the
rope was put about her neck. At the signal the ladder was pulled

away, and Mary Blandy paid the price of her crime.

Fetters and the like were mainly for confinement, but an implement which brought terror to its victims was the gauntlets. This device was feared as much as the rack and indeed they had much in common, for while the rack stretched the victim horizontally, the gauntlets pulled the joints vertically. It was a simple device, consisting of handcuffs joined by a long chain or bar. With the victim standing on blocks of wood, his back against a pillar or wall, the gauntlets were locked about his wrists. The connecting link was then hooked over iron staples high above his head, and the torture started as the blocks of wood were removed one by one.

This device was widely used in prisons throughout the country, though it is thought to have been introduced by Richard Topcliffe, the priest catcher mentioned in chapter 2. Topcliffe's men, searching for the priests' hiding places in Catholic houses, sought and eventually captured the man who had installed secret cavities behind panelling and even beneath fireplaces. He was Nicholas Owen known as Little John, a Jesuit lay brother whose capture on 23 January 1606 brought great satisfaction to the authorities hunting for those implicated in the Gunpowder Plot three months earlier.

Owen's skills in incorporating priest holes, and his knowledge of the scores of houses which contained them, had to be extracted from him so that a rich harvest of fugitive priests could be rounded up and executed. The Lieutenant of the Tower was ordered to wring the secrets from him, so Owen was taken to the White Tower dungeon and suspended by his thumbs. When he refused to talk, he was threatened with the rack and then subjected to the gauntlets with the torture intensified by heavy weights attached to his ankles, dislocating hip and shoulder joints. So severe was the treatment that, in the words of John Gerard, a fellow sufferer 'his bowels gushed out with his life' – though other sources report that Owen committed suicide in his cell. Whatever the cause, the lieutenant's records state: 'The man is dead – he died in our hands.'

Gerard, a Jesuit Father, was coincidentally nicknamed Long John, and his height posed problems for those putting him to the gauntlets in the Tower. The special warrant required where torture was involved directed the Lieutenant: 'You shall by virtue hereof cause him to be put to the manacles [gauntlets] and such other torture as is used in that place.' Gerard was secured to a pillar in the underground chamber but, upon removal of the wood blocks, it was found that the tips of his toes still reached the ground. The earth floor was dug away until he hung suspended by his wrists and his weight caused the iron

Curious old time military punishments

gauntlets to embed themselves deep in his flesh. Above the cuffs his hands swelled and throbbed so agonisingly, that only superhuman endurance sustained him as the hours passed and the damning questions were repeated again and again. Several times he fainted, whereupon men took the weight of his body until he recovered. Then they let him hang again.

His warder, Bonner, beseeched him to confess, in order to avoid further ordeal; but Gerard's resolve was strong. Time after time during the following days, he was subjected to the gauntlets, his hands now so maimed and helpless that Bonner had to cut his food for him and feed him like a baby. Between interrogations he was imprisoned in the Salt Tower, and it was from there, months later, during a respite from the questioning, that with the aid of his warder he escaped from his grim prison. Had he not got away, there is little doubt that he would have been racked, and burned at the Smithfield stake.

A military version of the gauntlets was used early in the 19th century, but because there were no pillars or walls in tented army camps, the culprit was suspended by his right arm from a high gallows-shaped structure. He stood with one foot on a sharpened wooden spike or picket, and so the punishment was known as picketing. It lasted for an hour, and then his arms were changed over and the soldier made to balance on the other foot.

## All fingers and thumbs

The Tower's inventory listed many instruments of torture but, in addition to government issue, there was also scope for the more inventive official to devise his own.

This certainly seems to have been the case when a deacon of the Protestant faith, Cuthbert Sympson, was arrested in 1557. At that time, during the reign of Bloody Mary, Edmund Bonner, Bishop of London was taking an active part in the persecution of Protestants. Sympson was a popular and energetic preacher who always attracted large crowds; if he could be forced to divulge the names of his flock – the bishop had ways of dealing with such heretics.

The Lieutenant of the Tower, Sir Richard Blount, firmly believing that old favourites are best, proceeded to marry the deacon to the Duke of Exeter's Daughter – the rack. Despite three hours of appalling pain, Sympson refused to submit. Sir Richard, while doubtless impressed by the man's fortitude, was determined to carry out Bonner's orders and forthwith devised a torture known as 'the arrow'. Sympson's forefingers were bound tightly together and a barbed arrow was pulled rapidly backwards and forwards between them until the flesh tore away and the arrow snapped. Still he proved obstinate, and at the failure of the arrow, the lieutenant subjected him to the crushing embrace of the Scavenger's Daughter.

Little is known of Sympson's fate. The fact that Bishop Bonner personally questioned him later implies that the brave deacon kept the names of his congregation to himself. It is known that Bonner placed the Pope's curse on Sympson, but he also conceded that the deacon had been the most patient sufferer of all who had come before him. The fate of Sympson's inquisitors however is well recorded. Sir

Richard died in 1564 and is commemorated by a kneeling effigy in armour, in the superb alabaster and marble monument erected to his memory in the Chapel Royal of St Peter ad Vincula in the Tower. Bishop Bonner, secure as a Catholic bishop could be in Mary's reign, fell from grace when the Protestant Elizabeth came to the throne, and was deprived of his bishopric in 1559. He died ten years later, a prisoner in London's Marshalsea prison.

Fingers are obviously vulnerable to barbed arrows; fingernails even more sensitive to needles inserted beneath them. This was a torture which a Catholic priest, Alexander Bryant, the martyr mentioned in chapter 1, was subjected to in March 1581. When arrested, Bryant, a handsome man of twenty-seven, was required to give samples of his handwriting, doubtless to compare with some incriminating letters held by the authorities. On refusing, he was denied food. 'Then it was commaunded to his keeper to give unto him such meate, drinke and other convenient necessities as he would write for, and to deny him anything for which he woulde not write', reports Lord Burghley, the Queen's councillor.

Days of starvation followed, in which Bryant ate the clay from his prison walls and licked the stones for their moisture. Later, still obdurate, he was racked and suffered needles thrust under his nails. And on 1 December 1581, with two companions, he was hanged, disembowelled and quartered at Tyburn. Nearly three hundred years later, on 25 October 1971, Alexander Bryant was canonized, a martyr to the cause.

Penny-winkis, pilliwinks or pinniwinks are comical names for far from comical devices, for these were the early forms of thumbscrews. Originally resembling nutcrackers, they evolved into the thumbscrews now displayed at the Tower. Simple in operation and design, they consist of two iron slots into which the thumbs were inserted, and an iron bar across the top which could be screwed down on to the thumbs a fraction of an inch at a time. An added refinement was a chain attached to the framework by which the victim could be led, or held by the links being hooked over a staple high in the prison wall.

Thumbscrews were frequently used in prisons all over the country, some models being designed to compress the fingers as well. These were known as pyrowykes or pilnewinks, and were first referred to in 1397. A later name for the thumbscrews was the thumbikins. The Privy Council of Scotland on 23 July 1684 stated: 'Whereas there is now a new inventione and Ingyne called Thumbikins, the Lords ordain that people put to torture shall have the Thumbikins or Boots or both applied to them.'

That extraordinary character Thomas Dalyell, a Royalist officer, who had once been a prisoner in the Tower, eventually reached Russia and became a general in the Russian army. He instilled strict discipline into the country's soldiery and on his return to Scotland in 1682 he brought Russian thumbscrews with him, using them on enemies of Charles II. One victim who later endured the torment was a Scottish minister, William Carstairs. He was accused of plotting to kill James II and his brother so that a Protestant could gain the throne, and it was therefore vital that he should be persuaded to reveal his accomplices. For nearly two hours he suffered the crushing of his thumbs, yet he remained mute throughout and staunchly kept his secrets.

Whether he was subsequently presented with the thumbscrews or not, somehow they found their way back into his possession – I hesitate to suggest that perhaps he couldn't get them off – and in 1689 he showed them to his new king, Protestant William III. His Majesty tentatively tried them on, admitting that the slightest pressure would have made him confess immediately. Nor did the King forget the device's persuasive ways for in 1690 he directed that they should be used on Henry Neville Payne, a conspirator against him.

As with other such instruments, thumbscrews were also used on women, and in particular on those suspected of witchcraft. The 1591 conspiracy involving Dr Fiennes, whose legs were so cruelly crushed in the boots, also resulted in the arrest of Agnes Sampson, a reputed witch. She was subjected to the pilliwinks and her thumbs were compressed until she divulged details of the plot against King James.

While not exactly a judicial punishment, mention must be made of the finger pillory, a device which utilised the fact that, if one's finger is secured while bent at the second joint as if in an 'L' shaped tube, it is impossible to withdraw it until released. A more detailed description of the finger pillory installed in the parish church at Ashby-de-la-Zouch in Leicestershire appeared in Notes and Queries of 25 October 1851. It consisted of two lengths of oak, each being three feet eight inches long, four and a half inches wide and two and a half inches deep. The lower board was attached to the wall horizontally and the upper board was attached to it by a hinge. In the lower board were a number of hollows varying in size, and at the inner end of each hollow a vertical hole had been drilled downwards. Corresponding hollows had been shaped in the upper board, matching those below when the boards were closed. The culprit's fingers were placed in the hollows of the lower board and the ends of his fingers were inserted into the holes up to the second joint. The upper board was then lowered and padlocked into position, trapping the fingers immoveably between the two boards.

Many churches used finger pillories to punish those who had caused disturbances during church services, and they must have been extremely effective. Other models were rather more portable, the device being mounted on a heavy wooden pedestal about three feet high. Rich carvings and decoration made it a handsome piece of furniture, though disobedient children or servants would hardly agree!

Wealthy families also found a use for them: the *History of Staffordshire* of 1686 related that in Beaudesart Hall was

... a piece of art made for the punishment of disorders that sometimes attend feasting in Christmas time etc, called the finger stocks, into which the fingers of all such persons as committed misdemeanours were put, servants and others of promiscuous quality, the device being divided in the same manner as the stocks for the legs, and having holes of different size to fit scantlings of all fingers.

And in an account of the fifteenth century customs of an Ashton-under-Lyne manor house, it is reported that 'at festivals in order to preserve as much as possible the degree of decorum that was necessary, there were frequently introduced a diminutive pair of stone stocks of about eighteen inches in length, for confining within them the fingers of the unruly.'

# 4 The Knife and the Whip

*All ye must do is to make a yawn*
*And thy mouth shall be skobit,*
*Thy tongue be drawn*
*Tied this way and that*
*Till naught can avail thee,*
*And then for good measure*
*Thine ears I shall nail thee.*

There was no real substitute for the knife when it came to punishing forgers, rioters, blasphemers, sheep stealers, puritans and similar criminals. Peasant or lord, clerk or politician, if the crime carried that penalty, the sharp blade carved its path. Sometimes the sentence of the court was enacted crudely and without frills; at other times it was performed with ritualistic ceremony.

One example of the latter was the penalty for striking a blow in a royal palace, such as the Tower of London. Any affray in such surroundings could endanger the monarch himself, and so the ancient punishment was death. In 1542, however, this was mitigated by a statute of Henry VIII whereby the offender was fined and imprisoned for life after having his right hand amputated. Interestingly, this Act was not repealed until the reign of George IV in the last century.

The amputation, as with most Court practices, followed a well defined procedure. After sentencing, the offender was brought in by the Knight-Marshal and met by the Sergeant of the King's Woodyard bearing a mallet, a large block of wood and some lengths of cord. The offender's right arm was then bound to the block in a suitable position. The King's Master Cook brought in the knife and gave it to the Sergeant of the Larder who positioned it on the wrist joint. The Yeoman of the Scullery had already arranged two benches on which the items of equipment were laid out, and he also tended a fire in which to heat the cauterising irons. Nearby stood a jug of water to quench the irons after use. The cauterising, or searing, irons were brought in by the Sergeant Farrier, whose task it was to sear the veins and stump.

The Sergeant Surgeon, using the mallet and knife, performed the amputation with the Groom of the Salcery standing by with vinegar and cold water in case the offender should faint. Then the Sergeant of the Poultry brought in a live cock and, using the amputation knife, beheaded the bird. After the offender's wound had been seared with the hot irons to seal it, the body of the cock was wrapped round the injured limb. The Sergeant of the Chandry and the Yeoman of the Ewry came forward with basin, ewer and cloths for the surgeon's use, followed by refreshments for all, offender included. The bread was provided by the Sergeant of the Pantry, and the Sergeant of the Cellar poured out wine, ale or beer as required. Each of the thirteen officials had his own task, so demarcation problems were avoided.

The loss of hands and feet was also suffered by those further down the social scale. In 1578 sheep stealers were punished by having both hands cut off, whilst three years later an author, Mr Stubs, and his printer William Page, also faced the knife. They had been found guilty of seditious writings, insulting to the Duke of Anjou, and to the Queen who intended bethrothal to that gentleman. Stubs and Page were sentenced to lose their right hands and on 15 November 1581 they were led from their cells in the Tower of London and taken to Westminster. There, on a scaffold specially erected in the market place, Mr Stubs delivered a long speech to the vast crowd of spectators and, immediately after losing his right hand, took off his hat with his left and shouted 'God save the Queen!'

Where the Tower is concerned, nothing is really new; events simply repeat themselves. Public concern is felt for the current wave of football violence, but the Tower has seen it all before. In 1222 a series of wrestling matches was arranged between the cities of London and Westminster, with a ram as the prize. The first match, held in London in a field by the Tower, passed off uneventfully, the home side winning decisively. However, the return match a week later presented a different picture. The Seneschal of Westminster had recruited expert wrestlers from far and wide, and such an unfair advantage incensed the London supporters. A running fight ensued and the Londoners were compelled to retreat.

Instead of resolving the dispute peaceably, Constantin Fitz-Athulf, Sheriff of London, assembled a mob and incited the rioters to march on Westminster. This they did and, led by the Sheriff, burnt houses and assaulted residents. Order was eventually restored, and the Mayor and officials of London were summoned to the Tower to be questioned by the Justiciar of England, Hubert de Burgh, later Constable of the Tower. Fitz-Athulf haughtily defended his decision and claimed the right to act as he wished, a high handed attitude which left the justiciar with only one course of action. The Sheriff, together with his nephew and another ring-leader, was arrested and, without word reaching the mob, they were taken to Tyburn and hanged the following day. Most of the rioters were rounded up, and punished by having feet or hands amputated by the executioner; others fled, never to return.

Within the range of punishments at the disposal of the courts were penalties involving the loss of ears and the slitting of the nostrils. Most of these were carried out at the town's pillory, an edifice erected in the market place and used for punishments described in chapter 5. The pillory's construction included a tall wooden post, and it was to this that ears were occasionally nailed. If the offender did not voluntarily tear himself free, the ears were severed by the beadle or the hangman.

Such a case occurred in 1552 when a man committed for fraud was pinned by the ears to the pillory in London's Cheapside. After the prescribed time had elapsed 'he would not rent his eare, so one of the bedles slitted yt upwards with a penkniffe to loose yt', as William Andrews recounts in his book. During the reign of Queen Jane, a man overheard speaking traitorously of Her Majesty had both ears cut clean off while a trumpeter played and a herald proclaimed the crimes committed.

Neither was rank any protection. Sir Robert Strange, accused of threatening the life of the Duke of Buckingham in 1628, was brought to the Tower and then whipped from Fleet Street to Westminster. There he had both ears cut off and was branded on one cheek. Another knight, Sir Peter Stringer, suffered even more. Found guilty of forgery, he stood in the Charing Cross pillory for an hour and then, as described in the *Weekly Journal* of 12 June 1731

> ... the hangman, John Cooper, dressed in blue like a butcher, came to him and with a knife like a gardener's pruning knife, cut off both his ears and with a pair of scissors slit both his nostrils, all of which Sir Peter bore with great patience. But at the searing with hot irons of his right nostril, the pain was so violent that he protested. His left nostril was not seared, and so he went from the pillory still bleeding.

Christian sentiments did not always intervene either. In November 1561 a man caught fighting in St Paul's Cathedral was marched to a post set up in the churchyard. There his ear was nailed, and later severed with a knife.

Perhaps the best known case is that of William Prynne, barrister, Member of Parliament and talented author. In 1632 he wrote a book abusing the theatre and condemning those who acted therein. As acting was a pastime of the Queen, King Charles' wrath was unrestrained and Prynne's enemies were delighted. After trial and a year's imprisonment, Prynne was fined £5000. Then he was taken to Westminster pillory and later to the one in Cheapside losing an ear at each and having his nose slit. His book was burned in front of him by the hangman and further imprisonment followed.

Iames Nailor Quaker ſet 2 howers on the Pillory at Weſtminſter. whiped by the Hang
man to the old Exchainge London, Som dayes after, Stood too howers more on the Pillory
at the Exohainge, and there had his Tongue Bored throug with a hot Iron, &
Stigmatized in the Forehead with the Letter: B: Decem' 17 anno Dom: 1656:

Flogging and mutilation

Freed later, he wrote more insulting pamphlets, this time attacking the bishops. These cost him another £5000 and he was sent back to the pillory. He was branded 'SL' for schismatic libeller, one letter on each cheek, by the public hangman, probably the appropriately named Gregory Brandon. This official burnt a letter in the wrong way round and had to burn it in again, a surgeon applying a plaster to relieve the pain. The stubs of Prynne's ears were then cut away before he was released from the pillory. After further imprisonment in different castles he returned to royal favour and in 1660 was appointed by Charles II to be Keeper of the State Records in the Tower of London at a salary of £500 a year, a position where his literary talents could be harmlessly employed.

In addition to the punishments inflicted on hands, feet, ears and noses, tongues also came in for their share of mutilation.

James Naylor, a Quaker who professed to be the Messiah, so outraged society and the courts, that it might well take less time to detail what was *not* inflicted on him. Pilloried at Westminster for two hours, he was then whipped through the streets by the hangman. Pilloried again for a further two hours with his crimes written on a board in front of him, he was branded on his forehead 'B' for blasphemer and his tongue was bored with a hot iron. Later he was sent to Bristol and conveyed through the streets seated backwards on a horse to the market place where he was whipped. Then, on his return to London, he was imprisoned with hard labour in Bridewell Gaol for an indefinite period.

Savage sentences were not confined to places south of the border: Scotland punished its criminals with the same cruelty. In the words of Nicoll's *Chronicles of Perth*

... last day of September 1652, twa Englisches, for drinking the Kingis helth, war takin and bund to the gallous at Edinburgh Croce, quhair ather of thame resavit threttie-nyne quhipes upon thair naiked bakes and shoulderis, thaireftir thair luggis were naillet to the gallous. The ane haid his lug cuttit from the ruitt with a refour, the other being also naillet to the gibbet haid his mouth skobit and his tong being drawn out the full lenth was bund togidder betuix twa stickes heard togidder, with ane skainzie threid, the space of half an our or thairby.

Another Scot, Lamont, wrote a more easily understood entry in his diary for February 1650 – 'Ther was sundrie persons in Edenbroughe that had their eares nayled to the Trone for bearing false witness, and one that had his toungue pearced with a hot iyron.'

And on 9 May 1729 – 'a woman was whipt down the city, nailed to the Tron, then had a bit pinch'd out of her nose with a new-invented machine, and was after sent to the House of Correction for thieving, house breaking and other wicked practices.'

The whip had been the most favoured instrument of judicial punishment since the days when the Anglo-Saxons wielded whips consisting of three cords, each knotted at the end. Throughout the centuries men and women were flogged for committing a wide variety of offences, the punishments taking place in prisons, at cart tails, or while secured to whipping posts. In 1530 the Whipping Act ordered vagrants 'to be tied to the end of a cart naked, and beaten with whips through a market town till the body be bloody by reason of such whipping.' Five years later another Act decreed that 'rufflers and vagabonds' were to be whipped till their bodies were bloody. For a second offence they would be whipped again and lose part of their right ear; further idling was punishable by death.

It was not until the reign of Elizabeth I, in 1597, that decency intervened and culprits were required to be naked only from the waist up. From that time too, the whipping post came into use instead of the back of a moving cart. It is doubtful whether the victim benefitted from this change, however, as it was easier to hit a stationary target than a moving one.

Many offences carried the penalty of whipping. In Devon in 1598, mothers of illegitimate children were punished in this way, as were the reputed fathers. Scottish pedlars who deprived English shopkeepers of trade, thieves, drunkards and blasphemers all received the lash of the whip. Eleanor Wilson, a Durham woman, was publicly whipped in the market place for an hour, having been found drunk on Sunday 20 April 1690. Similarly treated was a girl of nineteen who was found guilty in 1769 of obtaining goods under false pretences. She was stripped to the waist and whipped on market day.

The sentence itself must have been enough to terrify the offender – 'that you be taken from here to the place from whence you came and from thence be dragged, tied to a cart's tail, through the streets, your body being stripped from the girdle upwards, and be whipt till your body bleeds.' And when the sentence was delivered by someone as sadistic as Judge Jeffries, the hanging judge of the Bloody Assizes in 1685, it was even more severe. One can only shudder at his comments from the Bench – 'Hangman, I charge you to pay particular attention to this lady. Scourge her soundly, man, scourge her till her blood runs down. It is Christmas, a cold time for madam to strip. See that you warm her shoulders thoroughly.'

One man who was similarly scourged was James Bainham, a barrister who was accused of heresy in 1532. On the orders of the Bishop of London, he was put in irons and then in the stocks. Still obstinate, he was taken to the Chelsea home of the Lord Chancellor, Sir Thomas More where he was tied to a tree in More's garden, a tree More called 'The Tree of Life'. There Bainham was severely whipped and interrogated but he still refused to yield and was sent to the Tower. Sir Thomas More, usually a humane and compassionate man, described himself as 'the scourge of heretics'. He had Bainham racked and in that way persuaded him to recant his religious opinions. Later, Bainham regained the strength of his convictions and rejected the Catholic arguments. He was burned alive at Smithfield, two years before Sir Thomas More too was imprisoned in the Tower and beheaded.

Whippings were always a public spectacle and large crowds gathered around the whipping post or cart. Even punishments within prisons attracted scores of visitors eager to watch the barbaric spectacle. Wednesdays were the days looked forward to by the fashionable London gentlemen, for then they could stroll elegantly along to Blackfriars and the Bridewell Prison to watch the women being whipped before the Court of Governors. The President of the Court, Sir Robert Jeffries (no relation to the Hanging Judge), sat with a wooden hammer in his hand, while the prisoner, stripped to the waist, was tied to the post.

The whipping continued until the President thought sufficient and he would then bring down the hammer. The victim, and her waiting companions, would beseech incessantly 'Oh good Sir Robert, knock; pray, good Sir Robert, knock!'

An account from one victim in 1703 describes how:

> my hands were put to the post and Mr Hemings, the Whipper, began to noint me with his Instrument and had, I believe, about a dozen strings knotted at the end, and with that I had Thirty-Nine Stripes. I confess I could not forebear bawling out, but good Sir Robert knockt at last and I was freed from the post.

Some criminals, perhaps, deserved their harsh treatment; men such as John Holmes and Peter Williams. They were London grave-diggers who found it profitable to bury bodies, but more profitable to dig them up again and sell them as specimens to medical lecturers. When in March 1776 the remains of twenty cadavers were found in a shed in Tottenham Court Road, the two 'resurrection men' were tracked down and arrested. Both were sentenced to six months imprisonment and were whipped on their bare backs as they travelled through London's streets, much to the delight of the watching crowds.

Perhaps the oddest case concerns Mary Hamilton, alias Charles Hamilton, alias George Hamilton, Alias William Hamilton. This woman was accused of disguising herself as a man and marrying in turn fourteen of her own sex! The fourteenth wife, Mary Price, became suspicious after three months of marriage and, as recorded in the *Newgate calendar*, she 'compared certain circumstances with her married neighbours' and thus realised Charles' deceit. The court decreed − 'that the he, she, prisoner at the bar is an uncommon notorious cheat. We the Court do sentence her or him, whichever he or she may be, to be imprisoned six months and during that time to be whipped in the towns of Taunton, Glastonbury, Wells and Shipton-

Mallet.' This sentence was duly carried out in the bitter winter of 1746.

Market days in market towns were the best times and venues for whippings, ensuring the greatest number of spectators. Occasionally the culprit was not only punished, but also expelled from the town. In January 1812 a man was whipped through Kendal, Cumbria, for fighting and a few days later a sailor was similarly whipped right out of town for causing an affray during church service.

As was to be expected, erring soldiers were also subjected to floggings. In the Army the penalty was known as 'going to the triangle' or 'going to the halberds', since in earlier times three halberds were tied together to form the triangle to which the culprit was secured. The whip used was the cat-o'-nine tails, which consisted of a wooden or whalebone handle two feet in length from which nine long tails of thick whipcord extended, each with six knots along its length. The punishment was administered in front of the entire regiment, the fearsome weapon usually being wielded by the drummer, while the sergeant-major recorded each stroke in an official notebook. Also present were the regimental surgeon and his orderlies, for medical attention was essential after a hundred or so lashes across bare shoulders.

On 10 October 1731, Robert Blackman, a soldier stationed in Berwick-on-Tweed, was court martialled for making traitorous references to the King. He was sentenced to receive one lash from each member of his regiment and then to be drummed out of town. A member of a Guards regiment, absent from his place of duty in the Tower of London, was punished with three hundred lashes, and a dragoon was given the same number of lashes at Nottingham and a further three hundred at Derby, for treasonable behaviour.

An odd variation of this Army punishment was known as 'running the gantelope' or 'running the gauntlet'. The offender, stripped to the waist, had to pass between ranks of his colleagues who beat him as he moved along. To ensure that he didn't run too quickly and so minimise the punishment, a sergeant went before him, holding a pike or halberd reversed so that its point was directed at the culprit's chest. These savage punishments were gradually phased out but, even as late as 1881, floggings were administered within military prisons and the 1914 Army Regulations still permitted provost marshals to apply up to thirty lashes for certain offences.

In civil law, the whipping of female vagrants was abolished in 1791, and all women were spared such indignity and pain by the passing of the 'Whipping of Female Offenders Abolition Act' in 1820.

# 5 Entertainment for the Neighbours

*Pipe him to the top of town and never let him back*
*And if his wife is worthy too, stop her bawdy clack*
*With bridle and a tongue-piece and let her rot in hell*
*For with mouth ripped nigh to ribbons what shall she have to tell?*

Until the middle of the last century many punishments were carried out in public; from the finger pillory under the gaze of the church congregation, to an execution on Tower Hill watched by thousands of spectators. Few people could read or write, national newspapers were unheard of, and radio and television had yet to be invented. It was essential, therefore, that the public could witness the power of the law and thereby be deterred from committing offences. Many minor offences carried penalties which, while not necessarily painful in themselves, were nevertheless accompanied by indignity and humiliation. In modern parlance, shame was the name of the game.

This was further increased by having the penalty exacted in the offender's village or town because it gave the neighbours an opportunity to make their own contribution to the punishment. If the offender was at all unpopular, they would add insult, ridicule or worse. In extreme cases the court sentence included banishment from the village, when the culprit was 'blown out of town with a bagpipe', the spectacle providing much free entertainment. The more severe the punishment, the larger the crowd.

One village event that was always certain to attract attention was the punishing of a gossip or a scold. Women using abuse or generally not holding their tongues had their mouths stilled for them by means of the scold's bridle. There were several different designs, but basically it consisted of an iron framework in the form of a cage which fitted tightly over the head with eye holes and an aperture for the nose. At the front, protruding inwards, was a small flat plate which was inserted into the offender's mouth and the bridle was then locked into position about her neck.

Some models were quite painless to wear; others had large tongue plates studded with sharp pins or a rowel, a small spiked wheel, to hold the tongue down. These could cause appalling lacerations if the victim should attempt to speak.

On top of some bridles, a spring mounted bell heralded the approach of the scold and a fine specimen of this type is on display in the Tower. Many bridles had a chain attached to the front so that the victim could be led through the streets and then secured to the market cross or pillory. Ancient houses in Congleton, Cheshire, had a hook

Iron bridles for a scold's tongue

fixed to the side of the open fireplace and incessant nagging would provoke the husband to summon the town gaoler. He would bring the town's bridle which was fitted on the wife and attached to the hook until the lesson was learned.

Bridles, also known as 'branks', were first used in Scotland in the sixteenth century: the Statistical Account includes the report of a Monifieth woman who was convicted in February 1563 of 'ye presumful abuse and vyc of drunkinness' and was sentenced to be 'brankit, stockit, dukit and banisit ye haile paris' (branked, placed in the stocks, ducked and banished from the whole parish). And on 5 March 1648 Margaret Nicholson of Dumfermline had to stand with the branks on her mouth for two hours before noon on market day for her common scolding and drunkenness, to be a public example for others.

The device soon crossed the border, and many still survive in museums; Lancaster Castle has an excellent example in its collection of prison artifacts. The use of the bridle became widespread; Elizabeth Holborn was branked at Morpeth market cross for two hours on 3 December 1741 for scandalous and abusive language in the town, while Ann Runcorn rued the day she abused the church wardens as they ensured that all the inns were closed during Sunday service. With the bridle on, she was paraded through the streets accompanied by hundreds of spectators and, on her return to Congleton Town Hall, the bridle was removed in the presence of the mayor, magistrates, constables, churchwardens, and assembled inhabitants.

Men too suffered the branks. James Brodie, a blind beggar, was sentenced to death for the murder of his young guide, but caused so much commotion in prison that he was silenced by the branks. He was executed at Nottingham on 15 July 1799. Any citizen of Edinburgh guilty of blasphemy had to wear the bridle and in the year of 1560 'David Persoun, convicted of fornication, was brankit for four hours and his associate in guilt Isobel Mountray, was banisit the gait.'

Not all scolding women were branked. Some, as in Leicester in 1467, were ordered to be seated in the cucking stool before their own door and carried to the four gates of the town. In Cornwall the cucking stool was 'a seat of infamy where strumpets and scolds, with bare feet and head, were condemned to abide the derision of those that passed by.' It was referred to in the Domesday Book as *cathedra stercoris*, literally a close chair or commode, as this was originally used to increase the indignity. Later an ordinary chair replaced it. The culprit had to sit in the chair in the street or market place to be reviled by his more law-abiding neighbours.

An historian, Thomas Wright, noted that 'in 1555 the Scottish Queen enacted that itinerant singing women should be put on the cuck-stoles of every burgh or town' – a fate which also awaited common brawlers and scolders in 1562. Similarly, there was always a place waiting for Scottish ale-wives who sold bad ale!

Further south, by a 1512 statute of Henry VIII, carders and spinners

Ipswich ducking-stool

of wool convicted of fraudulent practices, were to be 'set upon the cukkyng-stole'. Later the name became synonymous with 'ducking stool', and both names were eventually applied to a punishment involving immersion in water. This punishment was not reserved for nagging wives, but was used for dishonest tradesmen, shrews, harlots and whores. Nearly all villages had ducking-stools and it was noted by an eighteenth-century visitor to Derby that 'there is a curious and very useful machine viz a ducking stool for the benefit of schoolding wives. A plan of this instrument I shall procure and transplant to Berkshire for the good of my native county.'

The ducking stool took many forms, depending on local workmen and conditions. Some chairs were wooden, intricately carved with devils, scolds, and poetic quotations; others were of elaborately shaped wrought iron. The lack of a national ducking stool factory meant that villages designed their own, based on those seen in nearby towns and coupled with the resourcefulness of their own blacksmith and carpenter.

One stool was described as an armchair fastened to the end of two parallel beams fifteen feet long. The chair was on an axle so that the person on it remained horizontal even when the beams, balanced on a post by river or pond, were raised and lowered like a see-saw.

Another model consisted of a tall vertical post with a swing arm at the top. From one end of the arm was suspended a chair; a rope at the other end allowed the chair, duly weighted by a scold or suchlike, to be ducked. The vertical post was either fixed in the river bank or mounted on a small wheeled trolley, and this type was known as a 'treebucket' or 'trebuchet' because of its resemblance to an immense catapult of that name which was used to hurl boulders over castle walls. In villages situated by rivers, the chair was hung by a pulley attached to a beam in the centre of the bridge arch, so it was always ready for use. Yet another type of ducking stool was known as a tumbril or scolding cart, for it comprised a pair of fifteen foot long shafts, with two wheels on an axle fixed about three feet from one end. On the short end was mounted the chair, and on the other end long ropes were attached.

With the scold in the chair, the tumbril was pushed into the pond. The operators, still on dry land, would release the shafts, plunging the scold backwards into the water as the shafts flew upwards. After a suitable period of immersion the shafts were pulled down again by means of the ropes. One such tumbril existed at Wootton Bassett, Wiltshire and bore the date 1686 on its oak frame.

The ducking stool went under many different names, trebuchet, tumbril, timbrell, gumstole, coqueen stole or cucking stool. Research into parish accounts reveals the cost of these 'engines of punishment'. When Southam, in Warwickshire, had to install one in 1718, a man who visited Daventry to draw a copy of its chair charged 3s 2d. The carpenter asked for £1 1s 8d for material and labour, and the painter wanted 10s for his additional designs. The ironwork was made by the blacksmith for 4s 6d, the fee for carrying it to its final site was 2s 6d, and last but not least a further 9s 6d had to be expended to deepen the village pond.

These devices, once installed, were put to frequent use; as the records show: at the Leeds Quarter Sessions in July 1694, it was ordered that Anne, wife of Phillip Saul, being a woman of lewd behaviour, be ducked for making daily strife and discord amongst her neighbours. Similar orders were made against Jane Miller and Elizabeth Wooler.

Katherine Hall and Margaret Robinson were ducked at Wakefield in 1692 'by reason of their daily scolding and chydering, the one with the other.' Also in that town's Sessions of 5 October 1671, there appears:

> Forasmuch as Jane, wife of William Farrett, shoemaker, stands indicted for a common scold, to the great annoyance and disturbance of her neighbours. It is therefore ordered that she should be openly ducked, and ducked three times over the head and ears by the constables of Selby, for which this call be their warrant.

One husband in Kirkby, Yorkshire, got a nasty surprise when he applied to the magistrate to have his wife punished. The official decided that both were equally to blame and so, back to back, husband and wife were chaired by the constable, cheered by the onlookers, and plunged into the cold waters of the pond.

It wasn't always just a quaint village custom. Old scores were paid off and panic could follow indignity as the chair and its occupant were held under much longer than was safe. Indeed, on rare occasions deaths did occur, as happened at Nottingham in 1731. The town's chair consisted of a box large enough to accommodate two offenders at once, their heads protruding through holes in the sides. On this occasion a 'female of bad repute' was installed in it and, left to the mercy of the mob, was ducked so severely that she drowned. The mayor was later arrested and prosecuted, and the ducking stool was destroyed.

The last recorded case in which the ducking stool was used in England was in 1809 at Leominster, Herefordshire. Jenny Pipes, alias Jane Corran, was first paraded through the streets on the ducking stool, a singularly fine machine mounted on a trolley which ran on four inch wheels. On the centre post, three feet high, was fixed the see-saw like twenty-six foot beam, ensuring deep water for the culprit and dry feet for the constables. After the well attended parade, Jenny was trundled to the river near Kenwater Bridge and soundly soaked. It seems not to have really cured her, for the bailiff reported that her first words after her release were oaths and curses directed at the magistrates! In 1817 Sarah Leeke, also from Leominster, occupied the same chair as Jenny and would have suffered the same fate, but when the procession reached the river's edge, it was found that the water level was too low. Another ingenious device which provided entertainment for the public was the the drunkard's cloak, at least in Newcastle-on-Tyne, one of the few places in which this particular

Brank and Drunkard's cloak at Newcastle-on-Tyne

punishment has been recorded. Widely used on the continent, it was described by a witness in a book by Ralph Gardner in 1655:

> ... men drove up and down the Newcastle streets, with a great tub or barrel opened in the sides, with a hole in one end to put through their heads, and so cover their shoulders and bodies down to the small of their legs, and then closed underneath, called the new-fashioned cloak, and so make them march to the view of all beholders; and this is their punishment for drunkards and the like.

The tub had two small holes in the sides through which the culprit's hands protruded. These allowed him to take the weight off his shoulders – but woe betide him if his nose itched! The device was reportedly seen in America in about 1862, probably introduced there by the early English settlers.

The drunkard's cloak apart, it might seem that women were the main target of ridicule, but this was not so. Men accused of wife beating or vicious behaviour had to be shown the error of their ways, if not by a court of law then by their neighbours. This was achieved by the ancient custom known as 'riding the stang', basically a noisy procession involving the villagers banging tin cans and kettles, blowing whistles and horns, and sometimes even accompanied by a trumpeter. At the front, carried shoulder high, was a thick pole or ladder straddled by the offender, a figure of scorn to all as the deafening parade passed through the streets. Later the custom changed, and the man on the stang was a spokesman chosen by the villagers. He carried noise-making implements with him, usually a stick and a dripping pan, to add to the din. Every fifty yards or so the procession would stop and the spokesman would recite slanderous verses about the offender and his crime.

Effigies sometimes replaced the spokesman, one instance of which was recorded in the *Westmorland Gazette* in October 1893. Villagers expressed their indignation at the offender by riding his effigy on a stang, and a few years before, in 1887, the *Sunderland Post*'s roving reporter described a local incident in great detail:

> some excitement was caused in Northallerton last night by the celebration of 'riding the stang', which is to expose some one guilty of gross immoral practices and of breaches of sacred matrimonial rights. Some hundreds of people followed the conveyance, in which two effigies were exhibited, through the principal streets. At intervals a person in the conveyance shouted out in rhyme their object, and to state their intention to ride the stang three nights in succession and on the last night to burn the effigies on the green near the church.

The house of the culprit was visited during the parade and, if the offence was very serious, the offender's effigy would be burnt before his door.

In the south of England the custom was known as skimmington riding. Instead of a spokesman, two characters played the parts of the offender and his wife with one character wielding a ladle and the other a skimmer — much like a Punch and Judy show, except that Judy triumphed! Their dialogue provided a mobile drama reaching its crescendo at the culprit's house, after which the parade traversed the village. Among the crowd were some with brooms who ominously swept the doorsteps of others similarly suspected of maltreating their wives. The custom was countrywide as a Scottish poem of 1721 shows:

*They frae a barn a kaber raught*
*And mounted it wi' a bang,*
*Betwisht twa's shoulders, and sat straught*
*Upon't and rade the stang*
*On her that day.*

Wales, too, had its quota of wifebeaters and philanderers to punish, and there they rode the *ceffyl pren*, the wooden horse. The *Liverpool Mercury* of 15 March 1887 reported that the custom

> ... intended to operate as a wholesome warning to faithless husbands and wives was revived on Saturday in an Anglesey village near Llangefni. The individual who had drawn upon himself the odium of his neighbours had parted from his wife and was alleged to be persistent in his attentions to another female. A large party surrounded his house and compelled him to get on a ladder, carrying him shoulder high through the village, stopping at certain points to allow the womenfolk to wreak their vengeance on him. The amusement was kept up for some time until the opportune arrival of a sergeant of police from Llangefni, who rescued the unlucky wight.

The military had their own version, roughly similar to a hobbyhorse mounted on small wheels, the horse's body being of planks forming a sharp ridge (see page 35). For minor regimental offences the soldier would have to 'Ride the Wooden Horse' astride the ridge, arms bound behind his back. Pulled along by his colleagues, his plight was made worse by having muskets tied to his ankles to increase his weight or, as jocularly phrased, to stop the horse kicking him off!

Military records quote that on 7 June 1731 'a soldier in General Tatton's Regiment was whipt in the Abbey Court for marrying a girl. He who advised 'em to marry was set upon a Wooden Horse, with six pairs of spurs at his heels.'

The custom of riding the stang was still carried on in remote parts of the country as late as the 1890s, having been reported at Sutton, near Hull, in August 1877 and in Hedon in 1889.

Perhaps the most popular public method of humiliation was the stocks, many of which are still to be seen on our village greens. Portrayed in Anglo-Saxon books, they were in use for many centuries and changed little in design. The culprit sat on a bench or on the ground with his ankles or, more rarely, his wrists, locked securely between two horizontal boards, held in position by two uprights fixed in the ground. The authorities considered it so important that villages should have stocks that Acts decreeing this were passed in 1351, 1376 and 1405, the latter further declaring that the absence of stocks downgraded a village to a mere hamlet. There were many stocks within larger towns – and even a set at London Bridge which was still there in 1825. Naturally the Tower had one close by; the sixteenth-century historian Machyn reports:

> At St Katheryne beyond the Toure the ale wyfe at the Syne of the Rose, a taverne was set up for ettyng of rowe flesh and rostyd bowth – and four women was sett in the stokes all nyght till the hosbandes dyd feyche them hom.

In 1497, Westminster Hall stocks gripped the ankles of Perkin Warbeck, the impostor who claimed to be one of the murdered little princes, and he, like them, finished his days in the Tower. Even the high and mighty Cardinal Wolsey was similarly secured at Limington near Yeovil in 1500, for drinking unwisely at the village feast.

At the other end of the social scale, the newspaper *The Scotsman* reported on 2 April 1834 that a Kelso woman convicted of stealing clothes from a hedge was placed in the stocks, and the novelty of the spectacle attracted a large crowd. William Allan, found guilty of abusing his wife on the Sabbath – obviously not a crime on a weekday – spent twenty-four hours in the stocks, with a further two hours in the jougs, on market day. Another such offence, he was warned, would lead to his being banished from the town.

Wood stealers, vagrants, ladies of ill repute, card sharps and gamblers were all candidates for the stocks, as were those who refused to assist with the harvest. Sunday drinkers in Skipton had to be extra cautious, for when the church service was in progress the churchwardens would visit the inns looking for those who preferred tankards to hymn books. The wardens were led by the beadle in his cocked hat and gold trimmed coat, carrying his staff of office. Anyone found drinking would be locked in the stocks until midday – though occasions arose when the wardens themselves yielded to the temptations of their task and finished up drunk!

Great houses and colleges had stocks for servants and students, and prisons used them for restraint, Stafford Gaol having one ten yards long.

The last man reportedly to suffer in the stocks was a rag and bone man, Mark Tuck, who was found drunk and disorderly in the parish church, Newbury, on Monday 10 June 1872. A crowd of hundreds gathered the next day to witness his discomfiture as he sat facing the church with his ankles secured. His exclamations of relief as the church bell chimed the quarters were drowned by shouts of derision from the crowd and it was not until four hours later that he was released.

Rarely did anyone suffer real injury in the stocks, but merely damaged pride and chafed ankles, for they could use their hands to defend themselves from flying garbage. This was not the case, however, in the pillory. As described in ancient times, the pillory was an engine made of wood designed to punish offenders by exposing them to public view and rendering them infamous. Its construction was simple, consisting of a wooden post with its end sunk in the ground or, more usually, mounted on a platform. Fixed to the top of the post were two horizontal boards, the upper board hinged at one end to the lower. Each had three semi-circular holes cut in them, which matched up when the upper board was lowered. The centre hole accommodated the victim's neck and the outer two, being smaller, gripped his wrists. When the boards were locked together, the victim was held immobile, and indeed, the device's name was derived from a Greek phrase meaning to look through a door.

Some pillories were of a more elaborate design with a circular framework at the top of the post so that six or more victims could be pilloried together. Some could be rotated, while the posts of others were used as whipping posts and had two pairs of stocks positioned at the base.

There was a version called a thewe especially for women, probably incorporating a shorter post and smaller neck and wrist holes, for the benefit of offenders such as ale wives who had given short measure, common scolds and shrews. Pillories were considered so essential by the authorities, that villages not having one risked forfeiting the right to hold a market, a serious loss of trade in those days.

Although primarily punishment by humiliation, many cases resulted in injury to the defenceless culprit. Where the crimes had been particularly objectionable, the raucous crowds did not hesitate to pelt the prisoner with rotten vegetables, bad eggs and even stones and bottles – sometimes even causing the victim's death.

Mother Needham, an infamous procuress, was pilloried in St James's Street, London on 30 April 1731 and, although the beadles tried to protect her, she was pelted to death by a hail of brickbats. Ann Morrow, who impersonated a man three times in order to marry other women, was blinded by pebbles hurled by the mob.

The vast majority of offenders, however, were hurt only in their pride. The Lancashire county records of 1612 describe how Margaret Pearson, found guilty of witchcraft, was sentenced:

> to stand in the Pillorie in open market at Clitheroe, Whalley, Padiham and Lancaster, four market days, with a notice upon your head in great letters, declaring your offence, and there you shall confess your offence, and afterwards to remain in prison for one year without Baile.

Faulty bow-string makers were pilloried in 1385, sheep-stealers on the Isle of Jura in 1796 and, in 1664, authors of seditious books were similarly humiliated, having their books burnt in front of them by the public hangman. Daniel Defoe, author of *Robinson Crusoe*, also penned treasonable satires and, as well as being fined, was sentenced to stand in the pillory three times. This turned out to be no disgrace; a favourite of the public, he had flowers, not dead rats, thrown at him and garlands festooned his pillory.

Spreading rumours always led to trouble, in particular for a certain London maltman who, in 1382, told his customers that the mayor had been put in the Tower. He was pilloried and derided by an abusive crowd of hundreds. John de Hackford caused public alarm in 1327 by announcing that ten thousand men were preparing to unite and kill the London councilmen. He was imprisoned for a year and a day and sentenced to stand in the pillory for three hours every quarter 'without hood or girdle, barefoot and unshod, with a whetstone hung by a chain from his neck and a notice "False Liar" on his chest.'

The practice of putting offenders on view in the pillory continued until the reign of William IV, when it was abolished in 1837. As usual, the Tower of London was associated with its closing moments, for the last man to be pilloried was Peter James Bossy, found guilty of perjury, who stood in the pillory on Tower Hill, on 22 June 1832.

# 6 By Fire and Water

*Poor John Goose, poor John Goose*
*For him not the speed of the hangman's noose*
*But the crackle and spit of the ghastly fire*
*As inch by inch the flames grow higher.*
*Burn him merrily, cry the crowd,*
*So he hath no need of a burial shroud.*

Approaching the Tower of London, one crosses Tower Hill, with its traffic and office blocks, souvenir shops and ticket queues. But in the little park there, is a small cobbled area marking the site where, in front of tens of thousands of spectators, men and women were executed. Most of them were beheaded, some were hanged, but a few were put to death by fire. This was a convenient and economical way of dispatching wrongdoers, and was extensively used throughout the country for a wide variety of crimes.

One of the first to suffer on Tower Hill was John Goose, burned alive for heresy in 1475. Another, somewhat earlier, was Richard Wyche, Vicar of Deptford, also condemned for his religious views. Following his death in the flames, the public regarded him as a martyr and gathered his ashes as holy relics. This demand inspired Thomas Virby, the vicar of All Hallows by the Tower, to indulge in a little commercialism. Each night thereafter he replenished the ashes, adding scented spices to convince the 'customers' of the victim's holiness. So convinced were they, that they not only gave thanks in All Hallows, but offerings too!

At this apparent miracle, people flocked to the place from all over London, but eventually the authorities became suspicious at the seemingly endless supply of one man's ashes. Vicar Virby was arrested, his guilt being in no doubt when the ashes ceased to appear. He confessed and was severely punished for his sins.

Being burned alive was the usual fate of heretics, witches, and wives who murdered their husbands, and occurred in nearly all the big towns. The Protestant Bishops Cranmer, Latimer, and Ridley, condemned in the reign of Queen Mary, were imprisoned in the Bloody Tower, then taken to Oxford where all three suffered at the stake.

Several people perished at King's Lynn, Norfolk. In 1515 a wife, found guilty of murdering her husband, was burned in the market place, as was a witch, Margaret Read, in 1590. Two more witches suffered within the next few years and then, in 1791, the same market place witnessed the burning of a servant girl for helping a murderer.

One of the worst instances occurred at Lincoln in 1722, when

Burnt at the stake

Eleanor Elsom was found guilty of killing her husband. With her clothes and limbs thickly smeared with tar, she was also forced to wear a tarred bonnet, then dragged, barefoot, on a hurdle to the execution site near the gallows. After prayers she stood on a tar barrel positioned against a stake, to which she was secured by chains. A rope ran through a pulley attached to the stake, and a noose at its end was placed around her neck. When ready, the executioner pulled hard on the rope, strangling her as the pile of wood was lighted. The flames roared upwards fiercely, but it was half an hour before the body was totally consumed.

This barbaric method of executing women was in fact devised out of consideration for the female sex! Where the penalty for a man was to be hanged, drawn and quartered, it was considered publicly indelicate to butcher a woman in this way, so she was burned instead, the sentence being that she should be 'taken from hence to the place whence you came, and thence to the place of execution, on Saturday next, where you are to be burnt until you be dead; and the Lord have mercy on your soul.'

Often the executioner's pull on the rope brought death before the flames took hold, or the stool on which she stood would be pulled away, with the same result. Some victims were allowed to have small bags of gunpowder hung about their necks and waists to speed their demise, but even with merciful aids such as these, errors occurred at times.

Catherine Hayes, having killed her husband, was sentenced to be burned at Tyburn on 9 May 1726. As soon as the rope had been placed around her neck the fire was started but it burnt so fiercely that, when trying to pull the rope tight the executioner, believed to be Richard Arnot, had his hands badly scorched and had to retreat. It was impossible to extinguish the flames to tighten the noose, so more faggots were quickly thrown on to the fire to hasten the end of the burning, struggling woman.

Nor was gunpowder infallible. Where the faggots had not been piled high enough to reach the bags, or only smouldered whitehot around the victim's legs, considerable time could elapse before the exploding powder brought blessed relief. In England most witches were hanged, but in Scotland the penalty was fire. William Coke and Alison Dick, guilty of practising witchcraft in Kirkcaldy were burned to death on 19 November 1633, the following expenses being incurred:

| | |
|---|---|
| For ten loads of coal to burn them | £3.6.8 |
| For a tar barrel | 14.0 |
| For towes [tinder] | 6.0 |
| To him that brought the Executioner | £2.18.0 |
| To the Executioner for his Pains [!] | £8.14.0 |
| For his expenses here | 16.4 |
| For one to go to Tinmouth for the Laird | 6.0 |
| | ———— |
| | £17.1.0 |

Things were rather cheaper in Canterbury a century earlier, as the corporation records show: 'Paid 14s 8d the expense of bringing a heretic from London; and for one and a half load of wood to burn him, 2s; for gunpowder 1d; and a stake and a staple 8d, total 17s 5d.' Officials and the general public witnessed executions, and sometimes the Church was also represented. The parish register of Glamis for June 1679 records, 'Na preaching here this Lord's Day, the minister being at Cortachy burning a witch.'

Sometimes the 'witch's bridle' was used. This consisted of an iron ring nine inches in diameter, with a hinged opening, enabling it to be locked around the witch's throat. The ring was then attached to the stake by means of a chain and, if mercy was to be shown, the stool on which she stood was pulled away, causing strangulation.

One who died an unusually savage death on a pyre was Sir John Oldcastle, Lord Cobham. This aristocrat was accused of heresy and was held a prisoner in the Tower. With help from powerful friends at court he managed to escape but was recaptured four years later, in 1417. Condemned to death, he was drawn from the Tower on a hurdle to St Giles Fields and suspended by a chain about his waist. A fire was then kindled beneath him, and the heat and smoke slowly asphyxiated him.

All these executions received a great deal of public attention, and the jostling crowds would abuse the executioner, the victim, or sometimes both. On 5 July 1721 Barbara Spencer was found guilty of counterfeiting coins of the realm and, when taken to be burned at Tyburn, she was given time to pray. But, as reported in the *Annals of Newgate*, 'she then complained of the dirt and stones thrown by the mob behind her, which prevented her thinking sedately on her future. One time she was quite beat down by them.'

These victims were only a few of the thousands who were burned alive throughout the centuries. Oliver Cromwell, for instance, was responsible for the burning of about two thousand people at Drogheda on 13 August 1649 while putting down an Irish revolt. And when some rebels escaped and took refuge in a church, this too was set on fire, leaving few survivors. So the inhuman penalty which started when St Alban died at the stake in AD 304, took its terrible toll until 18 March 1789, when Christian Murphy alias Bowman, a woman found guilty of coining, became the last person to die in that manner. A year later the law was altered, so that after 5 June 1790, women were no longer burned alive but were hanged instead.

The strongest person is susceptible to heat, and so it was employed as a test of guilt or innocence by the Anglo-Saxons. Ordeal by fire was almost a religious ceremony, and was based on the theory that if a man was innocent the good Lord would not allow him to be hurt.

Accordingly, before undergoing the ordeal, he had to attend church services for the preceding three days, eat nothing but onions and salt and drink only water. At the trial, a brazier held a bar of red hot iron weighing about three pounds, and the accused had to take hold of the bar and walk three steps before dropping it. A priest then bound the wound with a linen cloth, which was left in place for three days. If at the end of that time the wound had healed, the accused was declared not guilty, otherwise he was convicted.

This method was used until as late as the thirteenth century when a man named Gideon was suspected of practising the black arts and was acquitted 'by the judgement of iron'.

Heated iron was also used to identify criminals. To be a man of letters generally indicates one to be a man of much learning and integrity. But when the letters concerned are burnt into one's cheeks or hands, the very reverse is indicated.

Branding, from the Teutonic *brinnan*, to burn, was first used by the Anglo-Saxons and continued until the last century. The instrument itself consisted of a long iron bolt with a wooden handle at one end and a raised letter on the other end. An excellent example has survived in Lancaster Castle and was frequently used in the law court there. After being sentenced, the prisoner had his left hand secured in the holdfast, two iron grips attached to the dock. The heated iron was then pressed against 'the brawne of the thumbe', the fleshy base of the thumb, and the brander, after inspecting his handiwork, would call loudly to the judge, 'A fair mark, my Lord!'

That particular iron was used until 1811, although as recently as 1826 prisoners at the bar were required to hold up their hands so that any previous convictions would be evident.

The branding iron letters varied according to the crime committed. Under the 1547 Statute of Vagabonds, runaway servants and the like were branded with a 'V', and further attempts to run away were punished by the letter 'S' for slave. This system was not abolished until 1636. Fighting in church was classed as sacrilege, and those using weapons for that purpose had an ear amputated. Further offences brought the loss of the other ear, and then 'F', for fraymaking was branded on the cheek.

Coinclipping was punishable by a heavy fine plus branding on the right cheek whereas under an act of 1698, thieves would be burnt on the left cheek nearest to the nose. This was changed to a less conspicuous marking of the hand when evil doers threatened to burn the cheeks of innocent householders to confuse the issue! Those holding extreme religious views sported the letter 'B', blasphemer, on the forehead while publishers of seditious libels were branded 'SL', and those who sowed sedition had 'SS' burnt into their cheeks.

Edward Floyde, found guilty of treasonable remarks in the sixteenth century, was sentenced to be pilloried for four hours, whipped at the cart's tail, fined £5000, branded 'K' on his forehead and then imprisoned for life. Other letters used in branding were 'T' burnt on the right thumb for a thief and 'M' for malefactor or man slayer. Should the offence be repeated and therefore the letters displayed to the judge, the penalty was death.

Nor were women spared. Lydia Adler, no longer able to tolerate her brutal husband, killed him in June 1744. As her neighbours testified in her favour, she was found guilty only of manslaughter and was 'burnt in the hand'. Sarah Swarton, charged with slander on 16 February 1619, was sentenced to be whipped through the streets, branded 'FA' for false accuser, and was imprisoned for life. Branding was also popular in Scotland, as is shown by the case of Janet Robertson who, on 22 October 1648, for her profanity, had to be 'cartit and scourged through the town, and markit with a hot iron and banished from the paroche.'

A rather strange alternative amounting to a symbolic punishment was devised in the eighteenth-century. A visitor to the Old Bailey in 1710 described how, for petty crimes, a cold branding iron was used!

> Some prisoners do not notice in their terror whether the executioner is taking the iron out of the fire or from the ground, and accordingly set up a great screaming. But when they perceive that the iron is not hot they become silent all in a moment; this is the case most often with the women prisoners.

In 1726 prisoners who could demonstrate their ability to 'read like a clerk' were not treated as common criminals, but had the right to be cold ironed. On payment of 13½d, the branding iron was plunged into cold water before being pressed against their palms.

Military discipline marched in step with civilian punishment, and deserting soldiers were branded in the left armpit with the letter 'D', while trouble makers had 'BC' for bad character. Branding irons were not used; instead, the letters were tattooed using a mixture of ink and gunpowder, and the method of tattooing was described in military regulations as late as 1858. Branding ceased to be a penalty in civilian courts after 1829, and was totally abolished in 1879.

Just as heat was a good persuader, so was water, and the previously

mentioned ordeal by fire had as its alternative the ordeal by water.
This was also performed as a religious ritual and took place in a
church. The accused was escorted by two men to an iron or brass pan
of water. The escort had to confirm to the watching priests that the
water was boiling, and that a stone rested at the bottom of the pan. If
only a single accusation had been made against the offender, he had
only to plunge his hand in up to the wrist to recover the stone. If,
however, a threefold accusation had been made, a deeper pan was
used, necessitating an immersion up to the elbow.

The congregation had to fast before the trial, to sanctify
themselves, and were sprinkled with holy water by the priests. After
all had kissed a crucifix, they watched as the accused man withdrew
his arm from the scalding water, and the priests bandaged the injured
flesh. As in the fire ordeal, the accused would be judged innocent if
the arm healed within three days, but guilty if the flesh was still raw.

A water ordeal feared far more than that with boiling water was
one whereby the accused was immersed in deep water. If, without
swimming, he floated, the verdict was guilty. If he sank, he was
innocent, and, one hopes, quickly rescued! James I favoured this
method of resolving the question of guilt, especially where witches
were concerned. These poor wretches were 'swum', with left wrist
tied to right ankle, right wrist to left ankle; or left thumb to right big
toe and vice versa. They would then be lowered into a pool or river
by means of a rope about their middle. To struggle in self-
preservation was to risk staying afloat, the sign of guilt; few indeed
could deliberately try to sink and be acquitted.

Water was also used for executing poisoners and coiners. For those
crimes, however, the water, or sometimes lead, was boiling and the
victim was plunged to his death in a cauldron. The penalty was used
frequently in the Middle Ages and was brought on to the statute
books in 1531, during the reign of Henry VIII. Indeed, Henry himself
was conversant with this type of punishment and, as can be seen from
the display in the Tower, he had his war-horse armour superbly
engraved with scenes from the lives of St George and St Barbara. One
in particular portrays a 'brazen bull', a hollow bronze animal filled
with water with an aperture in its back. In this hole kneels St George,
partially immersed, while beneath the huge animal executioners with
bellows and faggots keep the fires roaring. Above, an angel hovers,
symbolically waiting for the soul of the doomed saint.

The statute of 1531 was primarily to deal with the case of Richard
Roose, a cook who, as reported in Holinshed's *Chronicles*, had put
poison into the yeast while he was working in the kitchens of the

Bishop of Rochester. Yeast was one of the ingredients of the gruel or porridge prepared for the household and for the poor, who were fed out of charity. At least seventeen people died, including Benett Curwen, a gentleman, and Alyce Trypytt, a poor widow.

The bishop escaped death, but Roose didn't. In the words of the act – 'by causing that detestable offence nowe newly practysed and commytted, requyreth condigne punysshemente for the same; it is ordeyned and enacted by auctoritie of this presente parliament that the said Richard Roose shalbe therfore boyled to deathe.'

And so he was at Smithfield, London, on 5 April 1531.

Other poisoners both male and female were similarly executed. A maidservant, found guilty of poisoning her mistress, was boiled alive in the market place at King's Lynn, Norfolk, and Margaret Davey died in the same manner, for the same crime, at Smithfield on 28 March 1542. Later, a man accused of counterfeiting coins was taken to Smithfield, fastened to a chain, and lowered several times into the cauldron until he died.

This act, 'whereby such as kill by poison are either boiled or skalded to death in lead or seething water', was repealed in 1547.

Some nautical crimes also carried the penalty of death by drowning. In the Middle Ages it was thought only fitting that those who committed crimes on the high seas, should be put to death in the sea, or the river. This method of execution was generally applied to pirates, as quoted by Holinshed in the sixteenth century: 'pirates and robbers by sea are condemned in the Court of the Admeraltie and hanged on the shore at lowe water marke, where they are left till three tides have overwashed them.' Similarly, Machyn's Diary for 6 April 1557 reports: 'there was hangyd at the low water marke at Wapyng beyond saintt Katheryns by the Tower of London, seven men for robyng on the see.' It is likely that the men were only chained to a stake rather than hanged by the neck, and so met death by drowning.

The spectacle must have been a dramatic warning to sailors manning the scores of ships that entered the port of London, for records show that over three hundred pirates a year were executed along the Thames. This practice continued from 1440, when two bargemen were hung beyond St Katherine's for murdering three Flemings and a child in a Flemish vessel – 'and there they hengen till the water had washed them by ebbying and flowyd, so the water bett upon them' – to 1735 when Williams the pirate was hanged at Execution Dock and suspended in chains at Bugsby's Hole near Blackwall on the Thames.

Even earlier than the fifteenth-century, women found guilty of theft were drowned; and many powerful barons possessed a drowning pit for women who committed crimes in the villages they ruled. For male offenders, there was the gallows. As drowning could be classed as a speedier death than slow suffocation by hanging, it was awarded as a sign of leniency. For example, in Scotland in 1556, a man was sentenced to death by drowning 'by the Queen's special grace'.

At Edinburgh, in 1611, a man was drowned for stealing a lamb, and on 11 May 1685 Margaret M'Lachlan aged 63, and Margaret Wilson aged 18, were overheard to state that James VII of Scotland had no right to rule the Church. Both were put to death by drowning in the waters of Blednoch. Earlier, Janet Grant was charged with theft at Gordonston and, on 26 August 1679, she was drowned in Loch Spynie.

Close proximity to water made execution by drowning easy, and there have long been suspicions that the Tower of London disposed of some of its unpopular guests in that fashion. Reference has already been made to the underground 'dongeon among the ratts', and there is no reason why, at high tide, the waters of the Thames could not have been admitted to the cellars of the castle's riverside towers to immerse the unfortunate occupants. Some ancient documents suggest that the Wakefield Tower could also have been an oubliette as its large basement, 23ft wide by 10ft high was part of an early watergate entrance to the castle.

One former inmate of the Tower of London who met her death beneath the surface of the Thames was Alice Tankerville. She and her husband John Wolf were suspected of piracy, and Alice was imprisoned in the Tower. The only woman known to have escaped from the state prison, she managed to get out of her cell and over the walls – but fate was against her. Later recaptured, she was the subject of Lord Lisle's state papers dated 28 March 1534 which tersely reported: 'John Wolf and Alice Tankerville will be hanged in chains at low water mark upon the Thames on Tuesday.'

# 7 Death by the Noose

*Beat my chest and kill me quick*
*For the hangman's noose is but half the trick,*
*Or make a leap and pull my feet*
*That this death of mine may be complete.*
*For I am in a mortal dread*
*To find myself half live half dead.*

Tower Hill has always been a busy place, crowded with local residents, sightseers and holiday makers, but for really big crowds one must go back a couple of centuries to the time when the Tower's prisoners were executed there. Hanging days were holidays; tradesmen and apprentices alike were given a day off work to attend the spectacle, and over 20,000 people would assemble to enjoy the drama. In an age when there was little or no entertainment and poverty and disease made life cheap, a hanging anywhere in the country was an event to look forward to.

A wide range of offences, from shoplifting to murder, carried the death penalty. Even rare offences, such as the one noted by Stowe in his *Annals*, incurred capital punishment: 'On 26 day of Septembar in anno 1564, beying Tweseday, ware arraynyd at yet Gyldhalle of London four persones for ye stelynge and receyvynge of ye Queen's chamberpot, combe and lokynge glasse . . .'

Most towns had gallows and they certainly used them; over 72,000 men were executed in Henry VIII's reign alone. Just as nowadays London is reputed to have the best cinemas and theatres, so in earlier days it boasted the best hangings, many of them multiple events attracting large crowds. The Tower Hill site was mainly used for the execution of noblemen, who were entitled to the axe rather than the rope, and the vast majority of common criminals were hanged at Tyburn, at what is now the junction of Edgware Road and Oxford Street, adjacent to Marble Arch. A stone set into the central road island there bears an inscription to that effect but, should the unwary

Iussit amor pietasq̃ sacram me tangere dextram
Cede loco pollex, cedere iuʃsit amor.

Executions at Tyburn in the time of Elizabeth I

not heed the traffic, yet another tombstone would be engraved 'Died at Tyburn'!

Tyburn Fields originally consisted of 270 acres of rough ground, flat except for a row of elms bordering a little stream called the Ti, or Ty, bourne. The elms are significant, for among the Normans this tree was the tree of justice, and elms are also shown on ancient maps of Tower Hill.

It is estimated that over 50,000 people died a violent death at Tyburn between 1196 and its last use in 1783, but as few written records were made or considered worth maintaining, the real total may be considerably higher.

Those destined for Tyburn Tree, as its gallows were known, were brought either from the Tower or from Newgate Prison, the latter situated where the Old Bailey Central Criminal Court now stands. The earliest transport was quite primitive, with the victim being dragged along the ground behind a horse but, as this method frequently resulted in his premature death, an ox hide was provided

*Vita, norma decens pariter mors iunxerit Vna,*
*Hac duo Thesea pectora nexa fide*

Drawing on hurdles to Tyburn in the time of Elizabeth I

for him to lie on. Later a rough hurdle or sledge was substituted and the condemned man was dragged the three miles to Tyburn through mud and filth, over the cobbled highway lined with jeering crowds. Later still a cart was employed, large enough for a number of felons together with their coffins, the hangman, and one or two clergymen. The English language was thus enriched with such phrases as 'in the cart' and 'gone west', the direction to Tyburn from the Tower of London.

There were always exceptions, of course. Earl Ferrers, found guilty of shooting his steward Johnson, was held in a prison room in the Tower which, incidentally, his ghost is still reputed to haunt. On 5 May 1760, dressed in a silver embroidered suit, he travelled in a splendid entourage consisting of constables, horse grenadiers and foot soldiers, two carriages, a mourning coach drawn by six horses, and a hearse with the coffin. So great were the crowds that it took the procession nearly three hours to reach Tyburn. We will hear of the Earl again later on for, as befits a Tower inmate, he made an important contribution to the science of hanging, albeit unwillingly.

The route from the Tower was probably via Great Tower Street, Eastcheap, Gracechurch Street and Poultry. From there it continued westward along Cheapside and Newgate Street, High Holborn, Broad Street, High Street and finally the length of Oxford Street (then known as Tyburn Road) to the Tree itself.

For the condemned in Newgate Prison, the formalities started earlier in the week on 'curiosity day', which was the Sunday preceding their final departure. In the prison chapel they occupied a black draped pew, near to which stood a coffin on a bench. The remainder of the congregation consisted of fellow inmates, friends, relatives, and any passer-by sufficiently curious to walk in. All joined in the hubbub in an attempt to fortify the spirits of those soon to be hanged.

As if the tension in the prison wasn't bad enough, a further ceremony took place that midnight, and today's visitors to the church of St Sepulchre, opposite the Old Bailey, will find inside one of the implements used. Attached to one of the pillars at the east end of the north aisle is a small glass case containing a handbell, part of a bequest made by Robert Dow, a merchant tailor, in 1604. For the purpose of preparing the condemned for the next world, Dow bequeathed an annuity for a bellman to visit the prison at midnight before execution day. At a window grating the bellman would ring the handbell loudly and exhort:

All you that in the Condemned Hold do lie,
Prepare you, for tomorrow you shall die;
Watch all and pray; the hour is drawing near
That you before the Almighty must appear.
Examine well yourselves, in time repent,
And when St Sepulchre's bell tomorrow tolls
The Lord above have mercy on your souls.
    Past Twelve o'clock!

The annuity also provided for the 'passing bell', the great bell of the church, to be tolled as the procession assembled outside the prison, with further prayers to remind them of their fate. Finally, in the words of Stowe, 'at such time as knowledge may be truely had of the Prisoners execution, the sayd Great Bell shall bee rung out for the space of a quarter of an houre so that people may knowe the execution is done.' At one time the news of the actual execution was transmitted by a pigeon which, on being released at Tyburn, flew back to Newgate so that word could be passed to the bellringer.

The crowds thronging outside the prison and lining the route almost defy description. The public holiday would not only bring out all the city workers and apprentices, but the gentry and aristocracy in their carriages, complete with wine and food hampers. The presence of such multitudes in turn attracted vendors of hot potatoes, fruit, and gingerbreads; men selling pamphlets bearing the victim's 'Last Dying Speech', and women peddling gin and other drinks.

This noisy rabble provided perfect cover for thieves and pickpockets. With crowds averaging thirty thousand, and sometimes five times as many gathering for the execution of a lord or a notorious highwayman, their harvest was rich indeed.

With the exception of those who were overcome by the realisation of their fate, many of the condemned men basked in the crowd's adulation, or hurled defiance at the jeers and catcalls. Like pop stars attending a rock festival, they dressed up in all their finery, and appeared dapper and elegant in new suits and gloves, with combed periwigs, and nosegays thrown by admirers. Only briefly did this fashion parade alter; the 1720s saw many condemned men wear nothing but their shrouds, probably to spite the hangman who would otherwise claim their clothing, but the practice soon reverted to its previous style of extravagant apparel. Unfortunately, during the eighteenth century, the overall effect was spoiled by the requirement for prisoners to wear the noose around their necks, the rope itself being twined around their bodies. This task was performed by one of the sheriff's men variously called the 'Knight of the Halter' or the 'Yeoman of the Halter'. The hangman also travelled in the cart, seated on the coffins, as did the Ordinary, the prison clergyman.

Along the route to the gallows, one or more stops were made for refreshments. For those whose execution procession started from the Tower, a drink to speed them on their way was provided at the Golden Chain, one of the three inns then existing within the castle's walls. This custom may have been the origin of the expression 'having one for the road'. The main oasis, however, was at the hospital of St Giles in the Fields, outside which they were 'presented with a great bowl of ale, thereof to drink at their pleasure, as to be their last refreshment in this life.' This custom ceased in 1750, although a tavern called *The Bowl* was later built on the site of the old hospital.

Meanwhile, at Tyburn, all had been made ready for the hanging. In the early part of the twelfth century the gallows consisted merely of two uprights and a crossbeam, capable of accommodating ten victims at a time. Obviously it could not cope with the crime rate and in 1220 Henry III ordered that a further gallows be constructed there. In those days doomed men and women, dragged on hides or hurdles, were forced to mount a ladder while the rope was tied to the beam above. After a prayer or a speech they would be 'turned off', ie, the ladder was turned so that they swung in the empty air. These executions were carried out one at a time, doubtless because simultaneous executions would require up to twenty ladders and, of course, twenty hangmen. The procedure was speeded up by the use of a horse and cart for both transport and 'launching pad'.

This type of vehicle not only allowed the crowds lining the route to get a better view of the condemned prisoners, but it also delivered them unmuddied and unbruised. Once halted beneath the gallows, the cart's other advantage became apparent. Up to ten victims at a time could be roped to the beam and then a quick smack on the horse's flank by the hangman would ensure the rapid departure of the cart, hanging the ten simultaneously. The cart method held sway in more ways than one for centuries, until superseded by the trapdoor system described later.

Gallows were further improved when, on 1 June 1571, the triple tree was brought into use. Also known as the three-legged mare, this was a triangular gallows with three uprights joined to each other by crossbeams, making it possible to hang twenty-four malefactors at once. As befitted such an important innovation, its first victim was not any ordinary footpad or highwayman, but a celebrity from the Tower of London. The Harleian manuscripts state: 'the first daye of June 1571 the saide John Story was drawn upon a herdell from the Tower unto Tiborn, wher was prepared for him a newe payre of gallows made in triangular manner.'

Among the unique inscriptions carved upon the walls of the Beauchamp Tower, visitors will note '1570 IHON STORE, DOCTOR'. This gentleman, a fervent Roman Catholic, attained great power in Mary's reign and was very active in the persecution of the Protestants. When Elizabeth became queen, Story escaped to the continent, where he obtained a lucrative post with the Customs at Antwerp.

But Protestant memories were long, and Parker, owner of an English ship, lured Story on board to inspect the cargo. Once Story was below decks, the hatches were battened down, anchor and sails were raised, and the captive was brought back to England. He was taken to the Tower, where he was tried and found guilty. Although about seventy years of age, he was sentenced to a traitor's death at

Tyburn. After hanging he was cut down alive and, it is reported, struggled with the executioner while being disembowelled. Hardly a Story with a happy ending.

The fixed gallows continued to be used for two centuries, and were replaced in 1759 with moveable ones which were assembled when needed and afterwards returned to store. On at least one occasion, in 1776, when the cart contained gallow-birds of different religions, a double gallows was used; two Jews were hanged on one beam, five Christians on the other.

But regardless of the type of gallows, the scene on hanging day was unchanged. Every window and balcony was packed; the whole arena was jammed with thousands of spectators who had spent hours waiting, drinking, fighting, and making merry. Grandstands were filled to capacity by those who could afford to buy a ticket from the proprietors, who were known as Tyburn pew openers. Just as ringside seats for a boxing match cost more when a championship fight is staged, so the grandstand owners raised their seat prices at the hanging of a famous or infamous felon. One owner, Mother Proctor, made a commercial killing (appropriately enough) at the execution of Earl Ferrers. So great was the demand for a good vantage point that she reaped a profit of £500.

But private enterprise was always risky. Mammy Douglas, the owner of the stands in 1758, increased the seat prices from 2s to 2s 6d for the hanging of Doctor Henesey, found guilty of treason. Despite protests the customers paid up, but their discontent turned to fury when, just as the doctor was about to be turned off, a messenger arrived with a reprieve! A riot ensued in which the stands were wrecked, and the efforts of the mob to substitute Mammy Douglas for the doctor were only narrowly frustrated.

Usually, however, the crowds waited patiently, listening for the distant roar which heralded the approach of the hanging procession, a roar much as one might hear on a state occasion today, but with a bloodthirsty undercurrent of excitement, growing louder and louder like a spark travelling along a touchpaper, and exploding into a frenzy as the cart actually came into view and stopped beneath the gallows. 'Hats off! hats off!' would come the cry, not as a mark of respect for those soon to die, but so that the spectators' view would not be blocked by the headgear of those in front of them.

The condemned prisoners were given a hearing as they made their defiant or apologetic speeches interspersed with jeers or applause depending on the crowd's mood or the victim's star quality. Then, as the assistant hangman swarmed up the 'tree' to attach the ropes, singing broke out, usually including the 51st psalm 'Have mercy upon me, O God'. Amid an atmosphere now electric, the victims were made ready. Where a solo hanging was involved, the condemned person gave the signal by raising his bound hands and pulling his cap down over his eyes, but with a multiple event no individual decision was practicable. Caps were pulled down, the cart was jerked away, and the victims were left swaying and kicking until they expired.

It should be pointed out that until about 1870 the rope was tied with a hangman's knot to form a running noose, and the victim died of strangulation as the weight of the body kept the noose tight. The saying 'Hemp is a herb of suffocating quality' was never more true, for death came slowly. Up to twenty minutes could elapse before breathing stopped. As a concession, the executioner would permit the victim's friends or servants to hasten death by pulling the victim's legs or thumping his chest while the jeering mob kept up a torrent of abuse directed at the hangman, casting doubt on his sobriety or parentage.

Last minute reprieves, such as Dr Henesey's, were rare indeed, and some alas came too late. Once, in York, the procession halted for a drink but the condemned man refused, being either impatient or teetotal. It was a decision he could have regretted, had he known, for only minutes after he had been 'turned off' a reprieve arrived!

One man who had more cause than most to blame the postal services, albeit unfairly, was William Townley, who was executed for burglary in April 1811 outside Gloucester Gaol. A contemporary Bath newspaper reports:

He was turned off a few minutes before two o'clock in the presence of a vast concourse of people, and apparently experienced no protracted struggle. The previous day, Friday, a reprieve was put in the Hereford post office, mistakenly addressed to the Under Sheriff of Herefordshire instead of Gloucestershire, after collection time, and so remained there until the next morning. At about 11.30 it was opened in Hereford and immediately the importance of its contents to the wretched object of intended mercy was ascertained, an express delivery was humanely sent off with the utmost celerity by Mr Bennett of the Hotel at his own expense, who started from thence at about 29 minutes after 12 o'clock and arrived at Gloucester a little after 2 o'clock; twenty minutes after the culprit had been turned off, and who was even then still suspended at the drop.

After the efforts of friends to speed the demise of the victim a bizarre custom was enacted. It was long thought that relics of the dead brought benefits of one kind or another to the living (many such relics are even now revered in cathedrals and other holy places). Women would rush forward to take the still jerking hand and touch it to their cheeks or bosoms as a cure for skin blemishes; children were lifted up to have the 'death sweat' applied to infected limbs; while even splinters from the gallows were considered certain cures for toothache.

A booming trade was done selling souvenir lengths of the actual execution rope. The more notorious the criminal, the higher the price charged by the hangmen who, not content with their perquisite of the victim's clothing, sliced the halter into small lengths for sale to the gullible public. After the execution of prison breaker Jack Sheppard in November 1724, the rope sold for 6d an inch. So great was the demand at some hangings that, in 1802 as the Yeoman of the Halter was peddling lengths of rope at the scaffold site for 1s a length, more was on sale round the corner for 6d, while Rosy Emma, reputedly the yeoman's wife, was doing a roaring trade with yet another cut up length in an adjoining alleyway.

By the eighteenth century it had become apparent that hanging led to too many cases in which the 'deceased' was cut down, rushed away by his friends and, with a surgeon's help, resuscitated. Other attempts to thwart justice involved a minor operation discreetly carried out in prison, as reported in the *Gentleman's Magazine* of 27 April 1733:

> Mr Chovet, a Surgeon, having by frequent experiments on dogs, discovered that opening the Windpipe Would prevent the fatal Consequences of the Halter, undertook to help the prisoner Gordon, and made an incision in his Windpipe; the Effect of which was, that when Mr Gordon had his Mouth, Nostrils and Ears stopt for some Time, Air enough came thro' the Cavity to continue Life. When he was hanged, he was perceived to be alive after all the others were dead, and when he had hung 3 quarters of an Hour, being carried to a house in Tyburn Road, he opened his Mouth several times and groaned, and a vein being opened, he bled freely. Twas thought, if he had been cut down five minutes sooner, he might have recovered.

Other attempts at revival involved galvanism, subjecting the corpse to electric currents. When this method was applied by Professor Aldin to murderer George Foster in 1803, far from resuscitating the dead man it resulted in another death, for the sight of the body having violent muscular contractions so terrified the Beadle of the Surgeons' Company that he died of fright!

So frequent were these cases becoming, that the authorities revised the method of hanging in order to increase the certainty of death. The cart was dispensed with and instead the victim stood on a trapdoor. It was known as 'the drop' and, when it was introduced on 5 May 1760, the Tower of London supplied its first victim, Earl Ferrers, mentioned earlier in connection with his splendid hanging procession.

A scaffold, or platform, had been built under the gallows and part of it, about a yard square, was raised eighteen inches above the rest of the floor. This hatch was covered with black baize and, when operated, was designed to fall until level with the floor.

As Tyburn didn't hang a lord every week, there was an immense crowd watching as the earl stood on the hatch. When the release was operated, design defects became immediately obvious, for the victim's toes still touched the lowered hatch; but as one observer recounted, 'The hangman, Thomas Turlis, pulled his legs and he was soon out of pain and quite dead in four minutes. Afterwards the executioners fought for the rope to sell, and the one that lost it, cried!'

The body was allowed to hang for an hour while the sheriffs and friends sat eating and drinking on the scaffold but it was quite clear that, as death came after some four minutes rather than the usual twenty, the new method was considerably more humane. Despite this, Tyburn reverted to the previous procedure, probably because of difficulties in perfecting the drop, and the cart was used until 7 November 1783 when, following the hanging of a robber, John Austin, the execution site was transferred to the area in front of Newgate Prison.

The Tyburn tree, no longer needed, was broken up and its timbers, together with those of earlier gallows, were sold to the landlord of a local tavern for use as barrel stands in his cellars. Some fragments are still preserved as holy relics by the nuns of the Tyburn Convent situated nearby.

The choice of Newgate as the new execution site was a shrewd one; the macabre procession was thereby eliminated and with it, the crowds that lined its route. The smaller area available outside the prison reduced the number of spectators to manageable proportions.

A further innovation coincided with the move to Newgate, and this was the re-introduction of the drop. Its hatch was now 10ft long and 8ft wide, large enough for the ten malefactors who were the first

New gallows at Newgate, 1783

to be hanged at the new site on 9 December 1783, by Edward Dennis and his assistant William Brunskill. Regrettably, the drop was still a short one, and this inadequacy was to go unrectified for over ninety years. Doubtless the authorities considered that four minutes strangulation wasn't too unmerciful.

Public executions continued throughout the country until 1868, when scaffolds were withdrawn behind prison walls. An account purporting to describe relatives witnessing the executions of their menfolk appeared in a Victorian guidebook and, whether factual or not, it throws interesting light on how executions were viewed in the early nineteenth century when they still took place for all to see.

The hangings occurred on a scaffold erected against the outer wall of Lancaster Castle, access being via an upper doorway leading directly on to the platform. After describing how the crowds had assembled from all over Lancashire and were now waiting impatiently for the spectacle to commence, the account continues:

The clock strikes 8 am and an official bids all present to be silent. The fated doors swing open and:
'Oh Lord, oh Lord!' exclaims a woman. 'There's the parson!'
'One – two – three – there's Jack – God bless him!'
'How lovely he looks! Dressed as if for a wedding!' sobs a woman.
'And there's Tom – he sees me – he sees me – God be with you, Tom!'
'And God bless them all,' cries another female, bursting into tears.
'Why, there's only four of them!' remarks a spectator with a

whining tone of disappointment.

'There must be six,' says another 'Six was the number, but there's only strings [nooses] for four, so two must have been reprieved.'

'Parson's shaking their hands – the Lord bless them!'

'How Tom stands, like a rock! What pluck! Doesn't shake a finger! Keep up, Tom!'

'Hangman's gone below!' cries a woman, her voice suddenly husky, and fixing her nails like a beast of prey in the arm of her companion. 'He's gone to draw the trapdoor bolt!'

'God bless them! God bless them!'

A jarring sound – the drop crashes down – a loud groan, sounding of hate and horror from a thousand hearts – now the shrieks and screams of women, then – the silence of the tomb. The scaffold is empty, justice is satisfied – and the crowd gradually disperses.

The last man to be hanged in public was Michael Barrett, a Fenian who attempted to free his imprisoned colleagues Burke and Casey by dynamiting the walls of Clerkenwell Prison. In the explosion many people were killed and scores injured. Barrett was hanged by executioner William Calcraft outside Newgate Prison on 26 May 1868.

The drop continued to be perfected, not without some bizarre mistakes, one at least resulting in decapitation. Several improvements were introduced; the inefficient hangman's knot was replaced by a metal eye through which the rope slipped smoothly and swiftly as it tightened, and the noose itself was lined with soft leather. Not only were new techniques devised, whereby death resulted from the instant severing of the spinal cord, but executioners of intelligence and humanity were selected for the task. By careful calculations involving the victim's weight, age and height and meticulous attention to the sequence of operating the drop, they ensured that death came within twenty seconds of the condemned person leaving the cell. The act ceased to be one of vengeance wreaked in public but one of necessary extermination in private.

The twentieth century saw fewer hangings than before, all behind prison walls, and in 1964 the death penalty was abolished except for offences under the Treason Act of 1351. The last criminals to be hanged were Peter Anthony Allen and Gwynne Owen Evans, condemned for murder. Tried at Manchester, they were executed at 8 am on 13 August 1964, Allen at Liverpool, Evans at Manchester.

# 8 The Fall of the Blade

*Let me dip thy kerchief in his blood*
*To save thee from an similar end.*
*Also look thou upon his pallid mask*
*And shudder with dread, my uneasy friend.*

Death by beheading was considered honourable by the Normans, and was introduced into England by William the Conqueror in 1076. The first recipient was Waltheof, Saxon Earl of Huntingdon, Northampton and Northumberland, the blow being inflicted by a sword. This type of weapon continued to be used at Scottish executions for many years to come but in England it was soon replaced by the axe, an ill balanced tool little better than a heavy chopper.

Yet despite that, execution by the axe was reserved for the nobility. Cold steel, rather than the rope, was considered swift and merciful – in theory. Among those who would disagree, were they able, would be the ill-fated Duke of Monmouth. 'Pray do your business well,' he warned the executioner. 'Do not serve me as you served Lord Russell. I have heard you struck him three or four times – if you strike me twice, I cannot promise not to move.' But move he did, for the axe descended on him five times and the final severance had to be made with a knife.

When the target was pitifully small and the avid crowd pitilessly large; when the axe was unwieldy and the scaffold boards slippery, often more than one stroke was needed. Mary Queen of Scots endured two blows as did Sir Walter Raleigh, while it took three blows to decapitate the Earl of Essex. And who can be sure that the first stroke rendered them unconscious?

The majority of such executions took place in London, the prisoners being brought from the Tower. During their trial at Westminster they had been escorted by the Tower's Yeoman Gaoler and warders, and the verdict was indicated to the eager crowds by the way in which the gaoler carried the ceremonial axe. This instrument, which is still in the Tower and is the badge of office of the yeoman gaoler, dates from the sixteenth century. Its burnished blade 20in long and 10in wide is attached to a 5ft 4in wooden shaft with four rows of polished brass nails down the sides, nails inserted in July 1746 when the axe was refurbished at a cost of one guinea (see Abbott, G., *The Beefeaters of the Tower of London* (David & Charles, 1985)).

If the sentence of the court was death, the axe was held during the return journey to the Tower with its edge pointing at the prisoner in

Axe, block and executioner's mask at the Tower of London

much the same way as in a military court martial, where the sword on the judge's table lies with its point towards the prisoner on trial if found guilty.

A typical execution started with the necessary paperwork: '11 August 1746, Herewith a Writ for the Body of Wm. Earl of Kilmarnock, from the Lieutenant of the Tower, and to behead him, and the like for Arthur Lord Balmerino.' The prisoner was then handed over into the Sheriff's authority and, still with his escort of yeoman warders, was marched up Tower Hill through the seething, jostling mob which often exceeded twenty thousand in number.

On the hill had been erected the scaffold, a 5ft high wooden platform with railings draped in black and boards strewn with straw. On the scaffold, near the waiting coffin, stood the block. Rectangular in shape, the Tower's block was about two feet high, though some were considerably smaller. At his execution in Whitehall King Charles I complained that his was too low, requiring him to lie almost flat and adding to the indignity of his fate.

The block was shaped to facilitate the executioner's task; midway along each of the longer sides the wood had been scooped out, wider on one side of the block than the other, so that the victim, face down, could push his or her shoulders in as far as possible. This positioned the back of the neck immediately above the flat area between the two hollows, with the chin resting in the narrower scoop, head poised above the basket of sawdust waiting there.

Some victims chose to have their heads fall into a scarlet cloth, but

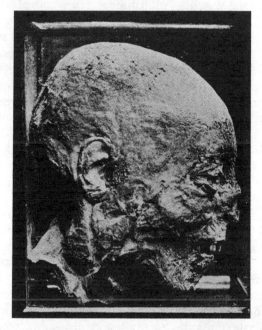

The head of the Duke of Suffolk

the sawdust which in 1554 cushioned the head of Lady Jane Grey's father the Duke of Suffolk, was impregnated with tannin, a chemical strong enough to preserve intact the skin and features of the head for nearly four centuries. On display until after World War II, it is now buried beneath the paving stones in front of St Botolph's Church Aldgate in London.

Once on the scaffold, the victim was given time to harangue the crowd, to ask the king's forgiveness, or to pray with the assistance of the priest at his side. Such speeches continued for half an hour or more while the executioner and his deputy waited impatiently. These two gentlemen were dressed sometimes in black, sometimes in white, with white aprons. Should they wish to hide their identities, masks could be worn.

When ready, the victim would have a brief conversation with the executioner, forgiving the man for the deed he was about to do, and bidding him strike true. A blindfold was optional for the victim who, kneeling in position over the block, would indicate his readiness by a pre-arranged signal, dropping a handkerchief or stretching out his arms. The axe then thudded down as often as necessary, accompanied by gasps from the watching multitude. Such was the force of the axe that the block itself became pitted and split, necessitating a new block for each batch of executions. The scaffold floor would sway and, to reduce this, efficient sheriffs had a wooden support installed immediately beneath the block in order to steady the boards.

But if the block didn't bounce as the axe impacted, occasionally the body did, springing backwards convulsively and twisting to roll on to its back as the head fell into the basket. It was then the executioner's duty to pick the head up by the hair, remove its blindfold, and at each corner of the scaffold, hold it high while shouting: 'Behold the head of a traitor! So die all traitors!' And just as a rabbit twitches after death, so the victim's eyes and lips continued to move, as if in mute protest.

That was the moment when the spectators nearest to the scaffold would crush forward to dip their handkerchiefs in the pools of blood soaking into the straw or dripping down between the boards. It was believed that blood so spilt or relics from the dead, especially from executed priests, had miraculous powers of holiness and healing. When the Jesuit priest Henry Morse was hanged and dismembered at Tyburn in 1645, the French Ambassador, the Marquis de Sabran and Don Antonio de Sousa the Portuguese Ambassador, were present to witness the barbaric ceremony and their footmen went forward to dip their masters' handkerchiefs in the martyr's blood.

The mummified remains of Father John Southworth, beheaded in 1654, are held and revered in Westminster Cathedral, London and when, during the same persecution, Father Campion was hanged drawn and quartered, another priest managed to obtain the fateful noose. One of Campion's arms, later displayed on a City gate, was taken down and kept by some of his fellow Jesuits.

Skulls of executed men were considered especially efficacious. The workers in the Royal Mint, within the Tower of London, were constantly exposed to the poisonous fumes rising from the crucibles and so, to combat disease, they were allowed to claim the skulls from over Traitors' Gate. It was well known that medicine supped from a dead man's skull was doubly effective. While the spectators at an execution were engaged in collecting the spilt blood, the body was placed in the coffin and, unless other disposal arrangements had been sanctioned, it was carried back into the Tower to be interred beneath the floor of the Chapel Royal of St Peter ad Vincula. The head was usually taken elsewhere for use as a deterrent.

Simon, Lord Lovat, when on the scaffold, nodded approvingly on reading the inscription on his coffin, and the selfsame plate, together with those of two of his fellow lords, Kilmarnock and Balmerino, now hangs on the west wall of the Chapel Royal. His states:

Simon, Dominus, Fraser de Lovat
Decollat April 9 1747
Aetet Suce 80

And he holds a record that few would wish to challenge, for Lovat was the last man to be put to death by the axe in England, the axe itself being on display within the Tower.

The procedure on Tower Hill generally functioned smoothly, well over ninety executions having taken place there, not only by the axe, but also by fire and the rope. The grim procession which started there in 1388 came to an end on 11 July 1780, when three people were hanged there for rioting, William McDonald, a one armed cripple, Mary Roberts, and Charlotte Gardner, a negress.

Within the Tower itself, on a private scaffold guarded by yeoman warders, and watched by a small, select audience, the heads of nobles fell. Five women and two men suffered this end. One of the men was William, Lord Hastings, whose opposition to Richard Duke of Gloucester, later Richard III, cost him his life. During a contrived quarrel in the White Tower on 13 June 1483, Richard uttered the fateful words 'I will not dine till I have seen thy head off!' Hastings was hustled down the spiral stairway to Tower Green and, without time for confession or repentance, was forced to kneel over a log and was brutally decapitated.

The other man was Robert Devereux, Earl of Essex, the proud and talented favourite of Elizabeth I, whose over-ambitious nature led him into a conspiracy to kidnap the Queen and gain power himself. Such treason could not be forgiven, and at about 8am on 25 February 1601 he was led from what is now the Devereux Tower to the scaffold site. He wore a gown of wrought velvet, a black satin suit with a small ruff about his neck, and a black felt hat. After asking forgiveness, and joining in a prayer, he removed his hat and ruff, and knelt over the block. Three blows were necessary to sever his head, though it was said that 'the first deprived him of all sense and motion'.

Earlier, on 13 February 1542, Catherine Howard, fifth wife of Henry VIII, suffered death on the Green. Improper conduct with courtiers and others was her crime, and so this queen of only one year, six months and four days, had to pay the price. With her on the scaffold, also to be beheaded, was her close companion Jane, Viscountess Rochford, who was accused of aiding and abetting the Queen in her immoral behaviour. Her fate was richly ironic for her late husband, Viscount Rochford, was George Boleyn, brother of Anne, and both had been executed six years earlier. George Boleyn had been charged with high treason and incest, and this latter crime had been testified to by his wife Jane. The swing of the pendulum had thus justly brought the swing of the axe to Lady Rochford.

The third queen to be privately executed was seventeen year-old Lady Jane Grey, the innocent puppet of the Duke of Northumberland. He had hoped to gain power through her, but the people favoured Mary as queen. Lady Jane's supporters marched on London and, in order to remove the cause of the conflict, Lady Jane Grey was tried and sentenced 'to be burned alive on Tower Hill or beheaded as the Queen pleases'.

Because the public execution of a queen could have adversely affected Queen Mary's popularity, the venue was changed, and on 12 February 1554 Lady Jane Grey was led from her place of confinement No 5 Tower Green, the home of the Gentleman Gaoler Nathaniel Partridge, to the scaffold. There her gentlewomen removed her gown, neckerchief and frose paste – a matronly head dress (the words later evolved into 'frow's piece' and eventually 'frontispiece'). After prayers had been said she knelt and on seeing the block asked, 'Will you take my head off before I lay me down?' As the executioner reassured her she tied the kerchief over her eyes. Then, reaching out, she exclaimed, 'What shall I do, where is it?' A weeping companion guided her and, as she bent her neck, the axe descended on the queen of nine days.

The axe did not spare those who were seventy-one years old any more than those who were seventeen, as Margaret Pole, Countess of Salisbury found out to her cost. Despite being the niece of Edward IV, she was accused of high treason by Henry VIII and, without trial or confession, condemned to death. On 27 May 1541 the courageous old lady was brought from her prison room to the scaffold and, defiant in her innocence to the charge, she refused to kneel over the block, for 'so should traitors do, and I am no traitor!' she proclaimed. The account by Lord Herbert of Cherbury continues: 'neither would it serve that the executioners told her it was necessary, so turning her head every way, she bid him, if he would have her head, to get it off as best he could; so that he was constrained to fetch it off slovenly.'

Even by the Tower's barbaric standards such butchery was to be deplored, yet the axe still continued to be an instrument of execution in the country for another two centuries. Its long list of victims ended in England with Lord Lovat in 1747, and in Ireland Father John Murphy suffered similarly in 1798 for supporting the rebel cause.

Although these were the last two to die by being beheaded, they were not the last to be beheaded! Two macabre episodes took place in the next century, one in Derby, and the last, fittingly enough, involving prisoners from the Tower.

In 1817 three Derbyshire labourers, Jeremiah Brandreth, William Turner and Isaac Ludlam, were accused of leading a revolt to overthrow Parliament, and were condemned to be hanged, drawn and quartered. Reputedly the Prince Regent remitted the quartering part of the penalty, but ordered that they should be beheaded traditionally by the axe. Two axes were made by a local blacksmith, modelled on the one still held in the Tower, the blades being 12in wide and 8in along their cutting edges.

The initial hanging took place outside the walls of Derby Gaol before a large crowd which included their fellow rioters. Cavalry and foot soldiers formed a wide circle round the gallows, and nearby was a long bench on which lay the two axes and a knife. A basket stood at one end of the bench together with two sacks of sawdust.

The three ringleaders were brought forward; nooses were placed around their necks, and their bodies hung for half an hour. The masked headsman, a strong Derbyshire miner, cut them down and, placing Brandreth's body face down on the bench, dealt the neck two prodigious blows, but still required to complete the separation by using the knife.

Holding the head high, he shouted, 'Behold the head of the traitor, Jeremiah Brandreth!', which so terrified the spectators that they fled in panic. The corpses of Turner and Ludlam were similarly maltreated and the poet Shelley, who witnessed the butchery, wrote a pamphlet condemning the authorities for their callousness.

The last beheading took place on 1 May 1820 when the Cato Street Conspirators were executed. Thistlewood, Ings, Tidd, Davidson, and Brunt had plotted to murder the Cabinet, capture the Tower of London in the ensuing confusion and seize the Bank of England. They were all imprisoned in the Tower and at their trial were found guilty. At 8am on the fatal day they were hanged outside Newgate

The Halifax gibbet

Prison, their bodies being left suspended for one hour. The dead bodies were then placed in their coffins with the heads protruding over the edge, whereupon a masked man deftly decapitated them using a knife. Rumour had it that he was a surgeon, so professional was the operation. The traditional shout drawing attention to the heads of traitors followed, and the corpses were later buried.

Mention was made earlier of the rarity of execution by the sword in England. The most historical execution using that weapon was that of Anne Boleyn within the walls of the Tower on 19 May 1536. No block was ever used with the sword, for the edge of the weapon would have struck the block's end before encountering the victim's neck. Anne Boleyn knelt upright to receive her death blow; the sword, travelling almost horizontally, was razor-sharp and finely honed. Death would have been instantaneous.

Axes and the occasional sword were alright in most parts of the country, but some towns liked to be different. For instance, a visitor to Halifax, Yorkshire, on a market day between the years 1286 and 1650, could have had more than just the opportunity to prod a cabbage or purchase a new jerkin. If the local crime rate was up to standard there was also the chance to take part in an execution. Gibbet Street led to Gibbet Hill where, on a stone base, the Halifax gibbet stood, a machine predating Dr Guillotin's similar device by centuries.

The chronicler Holinshed described it well:

There is, and has been, of ancient time, a law or rather a custom at Halifax, that whosoever doth commit a felony and is caught either hand habend or back berand, that is, having the stolen goods in his hand or bearing them on his back, or confesses the fact upon examination, if it be valued by four constables to amount to the sum of thirteenpence-halfpenny, he is forthwith upon one of the next market days or on the same day if it is a market day, to be beheaded.

The engine wherewith the execution is done is a square block of wood, of the length 4½ feet, which doth ride up and down in a slot between two pieces of timber that are framed and set upright, of 5 yards in height. In the lower end of the sliding block is an axe [blade] keyed or fastened into the wood which, being drawn up into the frame, is there fastened by a wooden pin. Into the middle of the pin is a long rope fastened, that cometh down among the people, so when the offender hath made his confession, and hath laid his neck over the base block, every man there doth either take hold of the rope, or putteth forth his arm as near to the rope as he can, in token that he is willing to see justice done. Pulling out the pin in this manner, the block wherein the axe is fastened doth fall down with such a violence that even if the neck of the transgressor be as thick as a bull, it would still be cut asunder at a stroke and roll from the body by a huge distance.

If it is so that the offender be apprehended for stealing an ox, sheep, kine, horse or any such animal, that same beast or another of its kind shall have the end of the rope tied to it and, on being driven away, shall draw out the pin, whereby the offender shall be executed.

That the head certainly did roll far from the body is evidenced by a local historian's account of a woman who rode past the execution site on horseback some distance away. As the axe block thundered down, its force propelled the severed head into the basket on the saddle in front of her. Constant recounting of this tale embroidered it with further details, describing the woman's horror as the head, missing the basket, gripped her apron and held on with its teeth!

The fearsome reputation of this machine gave rise to the saying 'From Hull, Hell and Halifax, good Lord deliver us'. Hull's strict bye-laws gave no favours to wandering vagrants, hell offered no redemption — and Halifax had the dreaded beheading machine.

The device is said to have been in use since the thirteenth century, but the first recorded execution in the town's register is that of

Richard Bentley of Sowerby on 20 March 1541. It was last used on 30 April 1650 when two men caught stealing thirty yards of cloth and two horses were tried by sixteen of the townsfolk. They were found guilty and, as stated in the court's records, 'Whereas by ancient custom and liberty of Halifax, the said John Wilkinson and Anthony Mitchell are to suffer death by having their heads severed and cut off from their bodies at the Halifax Gibbet; unto which verdict we subscribe our names.'

After that, the structure was dismantled but a fine replica now stands on the old stone base – with its blade securely immobilised. The blade from the original machine has survived, however, and is on display in the Piece Hall Pre-industrial Museum. It weighs 7lb 12oz, is 10½in long and 9in wide.

There is little reason to doubt the efficiency of this 'engine of justice'. One stroke proved sufficient, as opposed to the multiple blows sometimes required at the hands of the axeman. Another advantage was that the release of the Halifax blade was determined by the action of an anonymous multitude pulling the pin out, rather than one state-appointed employee. Democracy indeed! Holinshed mentions a machine similar to this one being used in Ireland as early as 1305, but gives no other details.

The efficiency of the Halifax Gibbet must have been realised by the Earl of Morton, Regent of Scotland, who watched it at work one market day in 1565. On his return to Edinburgh he had a similar machine constructed. It was known as the Scottish Maiden, from the Celtic *mod-dun* meaning the place where justice was administered. This device resembled a painter's easel and was about ten feet high. The victim's neck was supported by a crossbar four feet from the ground and held secure by another crosspiece above it. The two vertical posts were grooved down their inner surfaces where the sharp, lead-weighted blade would run. A peg held the blade at the top of the frame until required, when it was released by means of a long cord.

For 150 years it performed its gruesome task and over 120 victims were decapitated. Some were plotters involved in the murder in 1566 of David Rizzio, Mary Queen of Scots' arrogant secretary; but the most unfortunate of its victims was surely the Earl of Morton himself, who perished beneath its blade on 2 June 1581 at the City Cross in Edinburgh's High Street.

Later the machine added a father and son to its grim score. Archibald Campbell Marquis of Argyll, nicknamed 'the glae-eyed marquis' because of his severe squint, was condemned for high

The Scottish Maiden

treason, the sentence being carried out in May 1661. His son the ninth Earl of Argyll, also named Archibald Campbell, was sentenced to death for supporting James, Duke of Monmouth in his futile rebellion; 1685 saw the deaths of both men. Monmouth, as already mentioned, endured five blows of the executioner's axe on Tower Hill. Argyll, bowing his neck beneath the pendant blade, commented wryly that 'it was the sweetest maiden he'd ever kissed'. As the weighted axe thudded down, he achieved the doubtful privilege of being the last victim of the Scottish maiden.

This machine of death was dismantled in 1710, but its blade and other components have survived and are displayed in the National Museum of Antiquities of Scotland, in Edinburgh.

# 9 The Penalties of Treason

*Turn to a corner and retch if thou need.*
*'Tis naught but the first time ye see a man bleed.*
*Hereafter such duties will come all too easy*
*As for now, breathe ye deep and thou shalt not feel queasy.*

The worst possible crime in the eyes of the state was high treason, and this applied not only to those who plotted against king or country, but also to courtiers who dallied with the king's wife – as in the case of Anne Boleyn in 1536. It was appropriate that such crimes should merit the worst possible punishment. To be hanged by the rope or decapitated by the axe for committing 'ordinary' crimes was drastic enough, but high treason invoked the ultimate atrocity of being butchered *before* death – the penalty of being hanged, drawn and quartered.

The wording of the penalty requires some explanation as different interpretations have been made throughout the ages. The generally accepted meaning was that the prisoner would be hanged and cut down while still alive. A long incision would be made in his stomach, and his bowels would be extracted and burnt in front of him; that is, he would be 'drawn', as a chicken is before cooking. Next, he would be decapitated and quartered, his head and limbs being severed for display purposes. However, some confusion exists over the meaning or position of the word 'drawn', because the sentence of the court decreed that the prisoner should be 'drawn on a hurdle, or sledge' to the place of execution. This phraseology was used frequently, and an example is found in the notes of the trial of Doctor Archibald Cameron, charged in 1753 with helping the rebel forces in Scotland. Sentencing him, the Lord Chief Justice pronounced:

> You, Archibald Cameron of Lochiel, in that part of Great Britain called Scotland, must be removed from hence to His Majesty's Prison of the Tower of London, from whence you came, and on

Thursday 7 June next, your body to be drawn on a sledge to the place of execution; there to be hanged but not till you are dead; your bowels to be taken out, your body quartered, your head cut off and affixed at the King's disposal; and the Lord have mercy on your soul.

More accurately then, the details of the punishment were drawing, partial hanging, disembowelling, beheading, and quartering. No matter how it was expressed, it was an appallingly inhumane death, although on rare occasions mercy was shown, whereby deserving cases and those of noble birth were allowed to hang until dead before being butchered.

There was no mercy however for John Hall who, in the picturesque language of the fourteenth century, was accused of being an accomplice in the murder of an early Duke of Gloucester in 1399. The *Chronicles* of London record that:

> . . . the lordes had examined what peyne the same John Hall desyrved ffor his knowyng off the deeth off the Duk off Gloucestre; and the lordes seyde that he were worth the moste grete peyne and penaunce that he myght have. And so the Juggement was that the same John Hall shulde be drawe ffro the Tour off London to Tyborne, and ther his bowelles shulde be brent and affterwarde he shulde be hangid and quarterid and byhedid. And his heede y-brouht to the same place wher the Duk off Gloucestre was murdred.

Among the many other prisoners drawn from the Tower to their ghastly fate at Tyburn were Christopher Norton and his uncle Thomas – Yorkshiremen involved in a northern rebellion in 1570. Thomas suffered first, in the presence of his nephew; then the hangman executed his office on Christopher:

> . . . and being hanged a little while and then cut down, the butcher opened him, and as he took out his bowels, Christopher cried and said 'Oh Lord, Lord, have mercy upon me!' and so yielded up the ghost. Then being likewise quartered, as the other was, and their bowels burned, as the manner is, their quarters were put into a basket provided for the purpose, and so carried to Newgate where they were parboiled; and afterwards their heads were set on London Bridge and their quarters on sundry gates of the City.

The parboiling of head and limbs was necessary to preserve them for as long as possible when displayed, and was carried out in as barbaric a fashion as the execution. The *Annals of Newgate* relate how the hangman brought the heads in a dirty bucket and, picking them up by the hair, tossed them around playfully before putting them in a big pan and parboiling them with bay-salt and cumin seed. The purpose of these latter ingredients was, apparently, to deter the sea gulls.

The aftermath of the Monmouth Rebellion, when Judge Jeffries' Bloody Assizes exacted retribution by executing over 330 rebels in the Westcountry in 1685, resulted in similar gory scenes. An eyewitness' lurid account, as quoted by Sir Edward Parry, describes how some places

> . . . were quite depopulated, nothing to be seen but forsaken walls, unlucky gibbets and ghostly carcases. The trees were loaden almost as thick with human quarters as leaves; the houses and steeples covered as close with heads as at other times with crows or ravens. Nothing could be liker hell; caldrons hizzing, carkases boyling, pitch and tar sparkling and glowing, blood and limbs boyling and tearing and mangling, and Jeffries the great director of all.

The sheriff wrote to the Mayor of Lyme Regis in Dorset, ordering him to build gallows and provide nooses to hang the prisoners

> . . . with a sufficient number of faggots to burn the bowels of the traitors and a furnace or caldron to boil their heads and quarters, and salt to boil them with, half a bushell to each traitor, and tar to tar them with, and a sufficient number of spears and poles to fix and place their heads and quarters.

It is of some slight satisfaction to recall that the instigator of such legal atrocities, Judge George Jeffries, became a hunted fugitive himself three years later. When caught, he was locked up in the Tower of London in the custody of yeoman warder Bull, in whose house he was secured; though shortly afterwards he was transferred to much less comfortable quarters in the Bloody Tower. An old story records that whilst there he was sent a barrel of oysters, his favourite food. With eager anticipation he opened the barrel, only to find that it contained not oysters but a noose!

Jeffries' health deteriorated in the cold and damp conditions, and he suffered acute inflammation of the kidneys. He ate very little and on 19 April 1689, having wasted away to almost a skeleton, he died.

At times there were alterations in the execution procedure. The sentence was varied to include 'cutting off of privy parts' in addition to disembowelling, and on other occasions the hangman would extract the heart and, holding it up high so that the multitude could see it, would proclaim 'Behold the heart of a traitor!'

More than once the punishment was carried out with the aid of horses. In 1238 a squire broke into the royal residence at Woodstock, Oxfordshire where Henry III was staying, with the intention of knifing the King to death. In order to make an example of the attacker, he was sentenced to be torn limb from limb by horses, then beheaded and quartered. His limbs were to be dragged through the city and hung on the gibbet for all to see.

In Norwich in 1271 a violent quarrel broke out between the citizens and the priory. In the fighting that followed, two townsfolk were killed, the church was attacked, and the priory was over-run. Buildings were destroyed and many of the priory's inhabitants put to death by the mob. Henry III, with judges and forty of his knights, came to the town to sit in judgement. The prior was found mainly to blame, and all the church lands were forfeited to the king. The citizens were also found guilty however and paid a terrible price. Thirty-three of their leaders were executed: some were burned to death, some were hanged and others 'were attached to horses by the feet and dragged through the streets of Norwich until, after great suffering, they ended their lives and expired.'

The penalty of being hanged, drawn and quartered was not legally abolished until 1870, although it had not been fully carried out for many years previously. One of the last cases in which the actual words of the sentence were spoken occurred in 1781, when Francis Henry de la Motte was found guilty of passing details of British shipping to the French. Like the enemy spies of the twentieth century, he was held in the Tower of London, and after six months imprisonment was taken to Tyburn where he suffered a traitor's fate.

Mercy was shown, however, and he was allowed to hang for fifty-seven minutes before being cut down and beheaded. He was then disembowelled and, after his heart had been thrown into the fire by the scaffold, his body was buried in St Pancras churchyard in London.

## By arrow and bullet

Execution by the strangling rope and unwieldy axe brought death by degrees. Far more effective and merciful was death by the arrow or bullet. From the year 870, when Edmund, King of East Anglia, was killed by Viking arrows, to 1941, when a German spy was shot by firing squad, the armed forces have favoured these methods of execution.

Admiral Byng, defeated by the French in May 1756, was court-martialled for neglect of duty and sentenced to death. On 27 January 1757 at Portsmouth he was shot by a firing squad of six marines, five bullets striking his body. Death was instantaneous. A few years later, in July 1795, four soldiers of the 1st Fencibles Regiment were tried for mutiny and found guilty. They were taken from Musselburgh, Scotland to Gullane, some twelve miles away. There the ringleader, Alexander Fraser, was sentenced to be shot. The other three were ordered to draw lots, the loser to join Fraser in death. This inhumane gamble led to Charles M'Intosh and Fraser facing the guns of their fellow soldiers. After the execution the regiment was marched round the bodies in slow time.

Few people, however, are aware that when the sound of musket shots echoed through London's narrow streets on 18 July 1743, it was the sound of British soldiers killing British soldiers within the Tower of London. For first hand accounts of what actually happened, we have two men who played vital roles in the drama to thank: the Reverend Campbell, who comforted the doomed men until their death and afterwards published a heartrending description of the scene, and Colonel Williamson, Lieutenant of the Tower at the time, who kept a meticulous diary.

The story opened in the spring of 1743 when the eight hundred men of Lord Sempill's Regiment (later to become the Black Watch) were instructed to report to Musselburgh where they would be reviewed. The troops were not the common soldiery of the time but 'gentlemen highlanders', sons of wealthy landowners and farmers who had joined as militia men, volunteers called on for service only when required. At Musselburgh they were informed that the venue had been changed to Berwick-on-Tweed, and, on marching there, they were then told that King George II, never having seen highlanders before, wished to inspect them in London. The regiment set out and arrived in London on 30 April, only to find that the King had departed for Hanover. Rumours then spread through the ranks that, instead of returning to their farms and families, they were to be split up and sent to various parts of the West Indies on indefinite colonial duty.

These rumours, probably circulated by Jacobite insurrectionists stirring up trouble prior to their rebellion two years later, further demoralised the men who were already complaining about their living conditions in camp at Finchley. Their pay was in arrears; their uniforms were of poor quality, especially their shoes and plaids; and they even had to supply their own swords. By 17 May they were ripe for desertion, and a night meeting was held on Finchley Common. Although many returned to barracks, 109 men, led by Corporal Samuel McPherson, set off north at 1 am the next day. Later that day a further sixty followed suit but after a few miles they were persuaded by their officers to return. The remainder of the regiment was immediately moved to Gravesend where they embarked for Flanders.

The body of deserters, behaving as a well drilled and disciplined troop and causing no trouble at all to the public, marched steadily north. The authorities offered a reward of forty shillings per man captured in addition to the usual mutiny reward, and three companies of dragoons were despatched in pursuit, intercepting the deserters at Lady Wood near Brigstock, Northamptonshire. At 10pm on 22 May the deserters surrendered without resistance and, their numbers reduced to 101 due to sickness, were brought back under heavy guard reaching London nine days later. They were immediately taken to the Tower.

Normally prisoners lived in the houses of the yeoman warders within the walls, or in the small towers but, being so many in number, nearly all of the deserters were accommodated in the Irish Mint, buildings in the easterly part of the castle long since demolished. The Lieutenant of the Tower received daily rations for them – a pound and a half of bread, half a pound of good cheese and a pint of oatmeal porridge per man.

On 8 June the court martial started its proceedings in the Lieutenant's Lodgings (the Queen's House), trying twenty men a day. It was then that the men were approached by a stranger who, together with an officer, advised them that if they pleaded guilty no punishment would be inflicted. They took the advice, only to learn on 12 June that the three ringleaders had been sentenced to death. The warder, with an escort of two sentries, broke the terrible news to the condemned men, Samuel McPherson, Malcolm McPherson and Farquar Shaw. All three were aged about thirty, of good families and had, in fact, endeavoured to dissuade their comrades from deserting, but their petitions for mercy were rejected.

At 6am on 18 July 1743 Colonel Williamson, the Lieutenant, paraded the men on Tower Green, the open space at the centre of the castle where nowadays thousands of tourists stroll and picnic in the sunshine. The ninety-eight deserters were ordered to form a large semi-circle facing the end of the Chapel Royal of St Peter ad Vincula, and spaced out behind them were ranged three hundred men of the 3rd Regiment of Guards – ironically the Scots Guards – to control any outbreak of revolt.

The wall of the chapel which faces Tower Green is now pierced by five windows, but in the eighteenth century the right-hand, east window had been bricked up to present a solid wall. On that fateful morning, two planks lay on the rough ground in front of the wall and the three condemned men, wearing shrouds beneath their clothes, were marched on to the parade. They knelt on one plank and the two ministers Campbell and Paterson faced them, kneeling on the other plank to pray. After nine minutes of prayer, which all the highlanders joined in, the ministers moved away and the three were ordered to pull their caps down over their eyes. At this, in the words of the Rev. Campbell:

> . . . eighteen soldiers in three ranks (twelve for the execution and six for reserve) who had been kept out of sight for fear of shocking the prisoners, advanced on Tiptoe round the corner of the Chapple and with the least Noise possible, their Pieces already being cocked for fear of the Click disturbing the Prisoners, Sergeant Major Ellisson (who deserved a greatest Commendation for this Precaution) waved a Handkerchief as a Signal 'to present' and after a very short Pause, as they aimed four to a man, waved it a second time as a Signal 'to fire'. All three fell instantly backwards as dead, but Shaw, being observed to move his hand, one of the six Reserve advanced and shot him thro' the head, as did another to shoot Samuel McPherson thro' the ear.

The officers on duty, and even the hardened Scots Guards were visibly overcome; many were in tears as the bodies were stripped to their shrouds and gently placed in the waiting coffins. They were buried beneath a black unmarked stone at the south-west corner of the chapel, now part of the footpath traversed by countless tourists entering the building on guided tours. The condemned men could not be aware of the last honour they had been unwittingly granted. Within only yards of their remains lie those of Sir Thomas More, Queen Anne Boleyn, Lady Jane Grey and many others of noble blood; so the three highlanders rest in worthy company.

As for their grief stricken comrades, far from returning to their homesteads, they were marched to Gravesend and, from there, thirty were sent to Gibraltar, twenty each to Minorca and the Leeward Isles, and twenty-eight to Jamaica. A sad end to a sad episode of military history!

Enemies of the state however, were very different. During both World Wars many spies were captured and, after trial, were executed. Some were hanged at Pentonville Gaol in London. Others faced firing squads in the Tower of London, brought from Brixton prison on the evening preceding their execution. Each was shot by a squad of eight soldiers in the rifle range situated between the inner and outer walls, less than twenty yards from the house occupied by the author and his wife when resident in the Tower.

Eleven enemy agents met their end there during World War I, the first being Carl Hans Lody on 6 November 1914. He was followed by Breekouw and Müller in June of the next year, then Roos and Janssen in July. Roggin and Melin were shot in September; Buschman and Ries in October 1915. In December Meyer was executed and then Hurwitz in April 1916. All were buried in the East London cemetery, Plaistow.

In World War II only one spy was shot in the Tower's rifle range – Feldwebel Josef Jakobs of the German army, aged 43, who parachuted into this country on 31 January 1941. He landed at North Stifford in Essex, breaking his ankle on impact. He was put into Brixton prison pending his court martial which on 5 August found him guilty. He was then brought to the Tower and held in a cell on the top floor of the Waterloo block, the Victorian barracks which face the White Tower in the Inner Ward.

Early in the morning of 14 August he was escorted to the rifle range and, because of his injured ankle, was allowed to sit in an ordinary Windsor chair. A circular piece of white lint was pinned over his heart, and at 7.12am the eight man firing squad of Scots Guards took careful aim and fired. Five shots hit the lint, killing Josef Jakobs instantly. His body was taken for post mortem to the Tower mortuary, a small, forbidding room in the moat wall beneath the Tower Bridge approach road, and was then buried in St Mary's Roman Catholic cemetery at Kensal Green, London.

# 10  Dissected or Displayed

*Step to thy toe and hold thy breath*
*For the May-time night bears the stench of death*
*And creaking above thy very head*
*Swing the blackened corpses of Henry's dead.*

After all three types of executions – hanging, decapitation, and being hanged, drawn and quartered – the remains of the victim were still of value to the state. If a criminal hadn't benefitted society whilst alive, at least he could enrich it after death; he could be morally recycled, so to speak. After hanging, a corpse could be used to further medical science or displayed as a deterrent against crime. After decapitation, the body was permitted burial but the head could be placed in a conspicuous place as a reminder, as could the component parts resulting from a victim having been hanged, drawn and quartered.

Before 1752 surgeons had to obtain bodies for dissection by buying them, and they didn't enquire too closely into the source of the supply. In that year the Government passed an Act decreeing that 'for the better prevention of the horrid crime of murder, some further Terror and peculiar mark of Infamy be added to the usual punishment of death; after hanging, the Bodies are to be given to the Surgeon's Company for dissection.'

This exploitation of the horror felt by criminals at the thought of their bodies being cut up and analysed proved effective to some extent, for thereafter condemned men bribed agents or begged friends to retrieve their corpses and carry them away for burial before the surgeon's men could appropriate the remains.

The first man to suffer in this way was Thomas Tilford, a one-armed youth of seventeen, as the Newgate records for 22 June 1752 show:

Thomas Tilford, you stand convicted of the horrid and unnatural crime of murdering Sarah your wife. This Court doth adjudge that

The body of a murderer dissected according to the Act of 1752

you be taken back to the place from whence you came; and there to be fed on bread and water till Wednesday next, when you are to be taken to the common place of execution, and there be hanged by the neck until you are dead; after which your body is to be publicly dissected and anatomized, agreeably to an Act of Parliament in that case made and provided; and may God have mercy on your soul!

The records also detail the treatment meted out to Earl Ferrers, whose notable execution has been dealt with in an earlier chapter. After hanging for an hour, his body was placed in a coffin and conveyed by hearse to Surgeons' Hall, London. There 'a large incision was made from the neck to lower breast, and the throat was opened. The lower part of the belly incised and revealled, whereby the bowels were taken away.' It was later displayed to the public, remaining on view for three days before being removed for burial.

The lawmakers of the day were advanced in sexual equality, for women as well as men were subjected to this barbaric sentence. One lady who did not welcome this equality was Elizabeth Brownrigg, a workhouse keeper, who treated her charges so brutally that death resulted. Pleading guilty to the accusation of murder, she was sentenced to be hanged at Tyburn on 14 September 1767. Her body was then taken to Surgeons' Hall where it was dissected and put on display for all to see. To aid medical science her skeleton, suitably treated, was kept there for many years.

Another woman, Anne Green, actually benefitted from this practice – it saved her life. Charged with killing her new born baby, she was hanged at Oxford, but when her body was being prepared for dissecting, the doctors heard a whisper of breath in her throat and sought to revive her. With warmth and nursing she recovered and was able to speak by the next day.

So many cases of revival occurred over the centuries due to inefficient hanging techniques that as early as July 1587 the Barber-Surgeons' Company announced:

> ... if any body which shall at any time hereafter happen to be brought to our Hall for the intent to be wrought upon the anatomists of the Company, shall revive or come to life again, the charges about the same body so reviving shall be borne, levied and sustained by such person or persons who shall so happen to bring the body.

Not only was revival and nursing an expense, but they had also been deprived of a dissection!

One who survived without the surgeon's aid was John Bertindale, a man who was doubtless glad he had been a piper rather than a drummer. Hanged in 1634 outside the Micklegate at York, he was left on the gallows for an hour. He was then buried nearby but, because of his strong throat muscles, defied death. A passer-by saw the mound of earth moving and, with considerable bravery, investigated, digging the 'corpse' out. As the law had ruled that he was officially dead, he was not re-hung. He got a job locally and, as York Castle annals record, 'In York continued blowing, yet a sense of goodness showing.'

Where sentences did not include dissection, the bodies of those hanged were used as dire warnings to the community. At strategic points in town and country, at crossroads and near gallows, the bodies, smeared all over with tar to preserve them, were suspended by chains with a notice proclaiming their name and misdeeds. And there they would 'wave with the weather while their necks held' for months, or even years, causing the bravest travellers to spur their horses and hurry past at night.

Some authorities deplored dissection altogether, calling it a waste of a good visual deterrent. Giving evidence before a Commons Committee set up in 1816 to enquire whether hanging in chains led to a decrease in highwaymen and murderers, one authority declared that it did, 'for there are a couple of men even now hanging near the Thames where all the sailors must pass, and they ask why the poor fellows are there. Upon being told for murdering two of His Majesty's revenue officers, they go quietly about their seafaring business.'

As an alternative to chains, the heavily tarred body was sometimes placed upright in a close fitting cage or gibbet, a fine example of which is on display in the Tower of London. Being thus supported by the narrow bars, the bodies survived for many years until they rotted away, the bones dropping out through the bottom of the cage. This device was greatly favoured by Henry VIII, and the historian Stowe reports that over 70,000 laden gibbets dotted the English countryside during his reign.

Many instances of gibbetting were recorded in the Newgate annals. The arsonist James Hill attempted to burn down Portsmouth dockyard and after execution his body was hung in chains on Blockhouse Point by the harbour, where it swung for many years creaking in the sea breezes as rust attacked the shackles.

A notable case occurred in Scotland when the Reverend Thomas Hunter was seen knifing two young children to death. In the dock he heard the judge pronounce that before hanging, his right hand was to be cut off at the wrist; he was then to be executed, and hanged in chains between Edinburgh and Leith. The knife with which he had committed the murders was to be used to transfix his severed hand to the gibbet, above his head. On 22 August 1700, this terrible sentence was carried out.

Gibbetting continued for many decades and the last corpse to be exhibited in this way was that of James Cook. He was a Leicestershire bookbinder who was sentenced to death for the murder of a commercial traveller from London. After his execution on Saturday 11 August 1832, his tarred body, with its head shaven, was suspended from a gibbet 33ft high in Saffron Lane, Aylestone, near Leicester.

This gruesome sight attracted so many people each Sunday, including the inevitable roisterers, pickpockets and vendors of strong drink, that eventually the body was taken down and buried nearby. The practice of gibbetting came to an end when abolished by law on 25 July 1834.

Confusion exists in history books between gallows and gibbets. Their design was almost identical though the former supported a living body temporarily by a rope, whereas the latter supported a dead body for as long as possible by a chain. The word 'cage' also lends itself to more than one meaning; an alternative name for a gibbet, it also meant an overnight lock-up equivalent to police cells today. The word is also applied to a punishment cage for a living miscreant like the one used to punish the Countess of Buchan for supporting Robert the Bruce in 1306. After she had been locked in it, the cage was suspended from one of the towers of Berwick Castle as a warning to others who favoured rebellion.

To exhibit a headless corpse on a gibbet was not really practical so, when the verdict called for decapitation, the body was allowed to be buried and the head, being recogniseable, was displayed instead. Similarly, after a victim had been hanged, drawn and quartered, the head, torso and limbs could be exhibited for the public good. To obtain the widest publicity, these remains were paraded on pikes to the city gates or to prominent buildings and impaled as high as possible on suitable spikes.

Most of Britain's old towns and cities were walled – Newcastle, Lincoln, York, Oxford and Chester to name but a few – and their city gates were the obvious venues. The toll bars and gates of London were especially appropriate as all travellers had to pass through them, and Horace Walpole records that, on approaching Temple Bar, he saw new heads displayed on it, and men making money by letting spy-glasses at a halfpenny a look.

About the same time, a local historian described the Tower of London as 'the grim fortress from whose battlements hung the bodies of scores of traitors drying in the sun. The heads of many others grinned at the passers-by from the pikes upright along the tops of the walls, food for the ravens that fought for their possession till only a whitened glistening skull remained.'

In 1282 Llewellyn, self styled Prince of Wales, swore that he would invade England and enter London with a crown on his head. And so he did; though, as he had been slain in the battle, the crown was an ivy wreath and, instead of his neck, a pike held his head high. Through streets crammed with jeering crowds the procession wound its way to the Tower where the head was set up on the tallest turret, to be joined the following year by that of his brother David. Traitors' Gate within the walls had similar ornaments, one being the head of Sir John Barkstead, former Lieutenant of the Tower. A Cromwellian, he had fled to the continent on the restoration of the monarchy but was captured and executed. On 19 April 1662 his head was returned and displayed in the castle he had once commanded.

For over five hundred years everyone wishing to enter London on foot or by carriage from the south had to use the old London Bridge, the only bridge across the Thames. Sturdily built, with twenty arches, a drawbridge, and gatehouses at each end, it was the ideal place to display deterrents; and the spectacle of rows of skulls on the battlements of the southern gate house soon became one of the City's landmarks, if not an actual tourist attraction. Paul Hentzner, a noted German traveller who frequently visited London and the Tower during the reign of Queen Elizabeth I, remarked that on one occasion he had counted no fewer than thirty heads mounted on pikes as he crossed the bridge to the city.

The use of the bridge for that purpose started on 24 August 1305 when the Scottish patriot and rebel Sir William Wallace was hanged. After his body had been dismembered, his head was set on a pole on the bridge and his quarters were exhibited at Newcastle-upon-Tyne, Berwick, Perth and Stirling. Priests and paramours, knights and vagabonds; the bridge had room for them all. The Earl of Atholl was beheaded in 1307, and his body was burnt. As a sign of the king's cruel humour the Earl's head was fixed higher than the other skulls on the bridge, for at his trial he had claimed to be of royal descent.

The reactions of an actual spectator are always fascinating, and an eye witness account following the execution of Cardinal John Fisher in 1535 relates that:

> . . . the head being somewhat parboiled in hot water, was pricked upon a pole and set high on London Bridge. Here I declare the miraculous sight of this head which after it had stood there the space of fourteen days, could not be perceived to waste or consume, neither for the weather, which was then very hot, nor for the parboiling, but it grew daily fresher and fresher, so that in his lifetime he never looked so well. His cheeks were a comely red, and the face looked as if it saw the people passing by and would have spoken to them, which many took for a miracle.

Earlier in history, not even members of the royal household were exempt. John Smith, Groom of the King's Stirrup, and Stephen

Ireland, Wardrober in the Tower, met their end on Tower Hill in 1483, to be partially reunited on the bridge gate later.

One historic and tragic figure whose head was placed there was Sir Thomas More, executed on the orders of Henry VIII. His body was interred in the Chapel Royal of St Peter ad Vincula within the Tower, but his head would have decomposed in the weather had not his daughter Meg Roper begged it from the bridge watchman. Throughout her lifetime she kept it in her possession, not an unusual custom in those days. After all, the head is the person with the individual brain and mind, whereas the body is just the life support system, the back-up machinery common to everyone.

On Meg's death she was buried together with the casket containing the mummified head in the Roper family vault in the Church of St Dunstan without the West Gate, Canterbury, a vault now marked by a modern tablet inscribed:

Beneath this floor is the vault of the Roper family in which is interred the head of Sir Thomas More of illustrious memory, sometime Lord Chancellor of England, who was beheaded on Tower Hill 6 July 1535

Ecclesia   Anglicana   Libera   Sit

In August 1978 the Vicar, the Reverend Hugh Albin, and a number of archaeologists and historians entered the tomb and confirmed that the casket and its historic contents were secure and undisturbed, as were the accompanying coffins.

Most men are only buried once, but one who was buried twice, in vastly dissimilar surroundings, was Oliver Cromwell. First interred with pomp and ceremony fit for a king in the Henry VII Chapel within Westminster Abbey on 3 September 1658, he was left undisturbed for over two years. During that time Charles II returned to the throne and retribution was levied against those who had caused the execution of his father, Charles I. On 30 January 1661, Cromwell's corpse and those of two of his henchmen, Ireton and Bradshaw, were dug up and dragged to Tyburn. They were hanged from ten in the morning until sunset, decapitated, and their bodies were buried beneath the gallows.

The Times of 9 May 1860 reported the finding of bones during excavations in the area of the Tyburn scaffold and, as most bodies hanged there were carried away for burial, display or dissection, the bones discovered in such a public place could well have been those of

Cromwell and his companions.

Their heads were returned to Westminster, not to their superb tombs in the Abbey, but to be impaled on poles on the roof of Westminster Hall, the scene of Charles I's trial. Through over forty years of sun and rain the skulls stared blindly across the city until the great storm of 1703 blew them down. Reportedly, Cromwell's head was found by a sentry sheltering from the gale and it later passed into the possession of an antique dealer named James Fox who, in 1799, exhibited it to the public in London. An ignoble end indeed, no matter what the crime.

Another henchman loyal to Cromwell was Major-General Thomas Harrison. He was savagely dealt with, being hanged drawn and quartered. His head was spiked on Westminster Hall with the others, and his severed limbs were skewered over the city gates. His staunchly republican principles triumphed in the end, however, for his son escaped to America, where he settled and raised a family. In 1891, little more than two centuries after Thomas Harrison's brutal execution, his direct descendant General Benjamin Harrison was elected the 23rd President of the United States of America.

London was not alone in displaying heads, of course. When Perkin Warbeck proclaimed that he was really Richard, Duke of York, one of the Little Princes in the Tower, he gained sufficient support in Flanders to raise an invasion force. Landing in southern England, the small army was overwhelmed and captured, 150 men being hanged. Their heads were then displayed on poles along the coasts of Sussex, Kent, Essex and Norfolk, while Warbeck himself suffered death at Tyburn.

Scotland too adopted the practice. On 21 May 1650 James Graham, Earl of Montrose, was executed for supporting the Royalist cause. He was hanged on the high gallows in the Edinburgh Grassmarket while his bitter enemies the Marquis and Marchioness of Argyll gloated over the spectacle. Montrose's head, parboiled, was skewered on a spike on the top of the Tolbooth in the city. Eleven years later, in 1661, the Royalists had their revenge as recounted earlier, when the blade of the Scottish maiden descended ending the life of the Marquis of Argyll. Montrose's head was wrenched off its spike, to be replaced by that of his erstwhile foe.

Nor was that the end of the grim saga. The marquis's head remained in place for twenty-four years until the Scottish maiden embraced the Argylls again, claiming the marquis's son in 1685. In turn his head was parboiled, and replaced his father's skull on the Tolbooth spike.

# 11  The Executioners

*Give me a neck be it narrow or thick*
*And I shall have its measure.*
*'Tis nigh a pleasure to dispatch man thus*
*All cleanly done with but a minimum of fuss.*
*If thou would'st have me quicker be, just ask it.*
*Look now — thy head is in the basket!*

Who were they, those men whose job it was to hang and to hack, to burn and to flog? Were they highly respected officers of the Courts, or hated ruffians — skilled and professional, or clumsy and callous?

As with any official position that had existed for six centuries or more, all descriptions applied at one time or another, though in general the less savoury breed predominated until about 1870. Generally known as The Common Hangman, they had many other titles, official and otherwise, Finisher of the Law, Executioner-General of Great Britain and Apparator of the Necklace being but a few. Perhaps the most unusual was that recorded in the Patent Rolls of 8 July 1370, whereby John de Warblynton was appointed 'Marshall of the Prostitutes in the King's Household, dismembering evil doers, and measuring gallons and bushells in his Household.'

The early records are incomplete, but from the hangman with a stump leg who executed Lady Jane Grey's father-in-law the Duke of Northumberland outside the Tower of London in 1554, to William Calcraft who in 1864 hanged Franz Muller, the first man to commit a murder on a railway train, the 'finishers of the law' were far from attractive characters. Few could write, or even sign their names; at best they were unthinking and unemotional, at worst merciless and callous. Most drank heavily, got into debt and ran foul of the laws they enforced.

Executioner Cratwell indulged in a little robbery on the side and on St Bartholomew's Day 1538 was hanged on his own gallows before a vast crowd of spectators. Similarly, the previously mentioned hangman with a stump leg was, as recorded in Machyn's Diary for 2 July 1556, 'taken in a cart unto Tyborne for theft and hangyd, he wyche had hangyd many a man himself, and beheaded many a nobull man and quartered many others.'

A successor, Pascha Rose, met the same fate on 28 May 1686 as did John Price, executioner in 1714. Having been a seaman Price knew the ropes in more ways than one, and despatched many villains with brutal efficiency, but beset by debts he lost his job to William Marvell, an ex-blacksmith whose dexterous axe-swing later severed many a Jacobite head. Price was locked up in the Marshalsea, the debtors' prison, but he escaped and, while roaring drunk, savagely attacked and killed Elizabeth White, a gingerbread seller. He was condemned to be hanged and gibbetted, and William Marvell's smithy skills were utilised in constructing the necessary iron cage and gibbet chains.

Execution day was fixed for Saturday 31 May 1718 but by then Marvell had, in his turn, been dismissed for debt and drunkenness. So John Price, clad in a white shirt and carrying a nosegay of flowers, was turned off by yet another colleague, Banks, and his corpse in its new iron suit swung high above the heath.

Some years later, in 1735, John Thrift was appointed hangman, an unwise choice for he was a kindly, simple man temperamentally unsuited for such a job. On one occasion, in a nervous attempt to hurry proceedings, he hanged thirteen men at once but forgot to pull their caps down over their faces first. This was an appalling breach of professionalism. After the 1745 Jacobite Rebellion he was required to wield the axe on Tower Hill, and was so upset at the prospect that he mounted the scaffold and promptly fainted. Revived with a glass of wine, he almost broke down again but then, in tears, completed the task taking three strokes to decapitate Lord Kilmarnock. Despite his inadequacies he served for eighteen years, narrowly escaping execution himself following involvement in a murder during a street fight.

In the same way hangman Edward Dennis cheated the gallows in June 1780. He was caught wrecking a Catholic's house during the Gordon Riots and was sentenced to death. In gaol he was held in solitary confinement to protect him from the vengeance of his fellow prisoners. While he was there, he petitioned the authorities to allow his son to succeed him, in order to keep the job in his family. It was then pointed out to him that if this was agreed, the son would have to hang his own father! Because of the hundreds of arrests made during the rioting, Dennis was released so that he could carry out the executions, and proceeded to hang thirty-four of his fellow rioters.

To a certain extent, men such as these could hardly be blamed for their misdeeds. Despised and reviled by the public except when a particularly unpopular felon was to be hanged, executioners were unloved and unappreciated. The judge who delivered the barbaric death sentence was usually a lord, honoured and respected. Yet the man who carried out that sentence, although just as much a servant of the state, was pelted by the mob and pursued by jeering youths. Even after death, his funeral procession was likely to be abused and stoned.

Some hangmen were gentle and humane, like William Calcraft who bred rabbits and pigeons, though throughout his forty-five years of office he persisted in using the short drop method whereby the victim fell only two or three feet and therefore took about four minutes to die. He was once a cobbler, and his shop sign was displayed in Madame Tussaud's Chamber of Horrors for many years. A framed signboard measuring three feet by two, it announced W. Calcraft as a 'Boot and Shoe Maker, and Executioner to Her Majesty'.

Among his friends he discussed his victims in a quiet and sometimes satirical manner, describing how, when hanging the Mannings for murder, the husband showed fear, shaking as the rope was adjusted, whereas Maria Manning was 'firm as a rock, never flinching'. On duty he always wore his scaffold uniform which consisted of a black suit with gold watch chain, and a tall hat. Once, after carrying out a hanging outside Lancaster Castle, he was asked about the possible sensations experienced by those being hanged there. His reply, quoted verbatim in a booklet about the castle by Thomas Johnson in 1893, was obviously based on accounts of felons who had later been revived, and certainly seems to describe the likely events of such an appalling experience:

> Well, I have heard it said that when you are tied up, and your face turned to the castle wall, you see its stones expanding and contracting violently, and a similar expansion and contraction seems to take place in your own head and breast. Then there is a rush of fire and an earthquake; your eye balls spring out of their sockets; the castle shoots up into the air, and you tumble down a precipice.

Calcraft continued in office until the age of seventy-four, although his familiarity with the job led Charles Dickens, on witnessing one of his performances, to comment, 'Mr Calcraft should be restrained in his unseemly briskness, in his jokes, his oaths and his brandy.'

Others in the profession were showmen, like William Brunskill who, with his seven clients swinging rhythmically behind him, stepped forward and took a bow. On another occasion, as two churchmen were joining in prayer with the condemned men, Clench and Mackley, and while Brunskill and his deputy were busy adjusting the nooses, the trapdoor suddenly fell from beneath them without warning. The six hurtled downwards, the felons stopping abruptly halfway as their halters tightened, to die without absolution or blindfold. The other four men finished up in a struggling heap of arms and legs in the pit with oaths being emitted by at least two of them.

Oddly enough, a similar mishap occurred at Newgate ninety-nine years later when James Billington and his deputy were officiating at the last triple hanging in England on 9 June 1896. With humane consideration they worked quickly and deftly, masking and pinioning the three victims standing on the drop. Warbrick, the assistant hangman, was still securing the ankles of one of them when Billington, his view obscured by a prison warder, operated the trap release. Warbrick heard the bolts click beneath him and as the floor fell away he went down head first. Desperately, he clutched at the ankles he had been pinioning, and finished up swinging in the pit among the legs of the three dead men.

Throughout the centuries many hangmen carved a niche in history, if only by association with their victims, such as Richard Brandon who was believed to have executed King Charles I in 1649. As a boy he practised by decapitating dogs and cats, and when he made the big time, so to speak, and wielded the axe at the royal neck, he received as his fee '£30 for his pains, all in half crowns, within an hour of the blow being struck, and an orange stuck full of cloves, and a handkerchief from the King's pocket.' He spent all the money, and sold the orange for ten shillings on Tower Hill. He died a few months later, some say from remorse at killing a king.

When Robert Devereux, Earl of Essex, was beheaded within the Tower in 1601, his executioner was Derrick, a man whose name has been applied ever since to a gibbet-shaped crane. Another whose name became well known, if not famous, was Jack Ketch. His brutal execution of Lord Russell in 1683, whom he struck three times with the axe, and that of the Duke of Monmouth who was not despatched until after five blows, earned Ketch such notoriety that for centuries afterwards all hangmen were nicknamed Jack Ketch.

Many offences carried the death penalty and with the introduction of the triangular gallows at Tyburn, mass hangings became possible. The record was held by William Lowen who, on Friday 29 June 1649, hanged twenty-three men and one woman at the same time – eight on each beam.

It is small wonder that the executioners had nightmares, but none were quite as bad as those experienced by James Botting. In 1820, after only three years officiating, his health gave way and he was confined to his bed. There he had repeated hallucinations of the criminals he had hanged, all 175 of them seeming to shuffle across the floor, with white caps pulled down over their faces, and their heads tilted to one side in a ghastly procession of silent approach.

It was nine of Botting's victims who were noticed by the eminent illustrator George Cruickshank as, early one morning in 1818, he was passing Newgate Prison. There, rotating slowly, were the corpses of those who had just been executed. Two of them were women, hanged for passing forged one pound notes – a prevalent crime in those days – and the horror of their deaths for such an offence so incensed Cruickshank that he determined to protest in the only way he knew – by employing his artistic ability. In defiance of the law, he designed a banknote, embellishing it with skulls, leg irons, and the gruesome figures of hanged men and women. The pound sign was formed by a twisted rope and noose, and the signature was that of Jack Ketch.

A large etching of the note was exhibited in the window of a friend's shop near Newgate, attracting so much publicity that the police were needed to disperse the crowds. The authorities of the Bank of England, aware of the strength of public feeling, decided to defeat the real criminals, the forgers, by issuing coins instead of pound notes. Due to Cruickshank's efforts, the currency substitution deprived the gallows of many scores of victims, and within a few years forgery had become a rare crime.

On the occasions when the public sympathised with the victim, it was the hangman who initially suffered. Dublin's executioner disguised himself by wearing a hideous mask, and had a large wooden bowl strapped to his back to protect himself from flying missiles.

In London the hangman's safety was equally imperilled. As is reported in the *Public Advertiser*: 'On 20 April 1768, Turlis the Common Hangman was much hurt and bruised by the mob throwing stones, at the execution of three men at Kingston' – and again on 6 March 1769: 'a tradesman, convicted of perjury, stood in the pillory in Southwark High Street and was severely treated by the populace. They also pelted Turlis the Executioner with stones and brickbats, which cut him in the Head and Face in a terrible manner.'

Nor did the attacks come only from the crowds; violent prisoners also posed a threat, and again Thomas Turlis was a target, this time at the hands of a virago named Hannah Dagoe. Having arrived at the gallows, this lady not only got her arms free but, flinging gloves, bonnet and coat into the crowd to deprive Turlis of his rightful dues, she cursed and struggled so wildly that he was all but thrown out of the cart. He overpowered her with difficulty whereupon, instead of giving the signal that she was ready to be turned off, Hannah suddenly hurled herself off the cart, to die before it could be drawn away.

It may be thought that the pay made the risks acceptable, but this

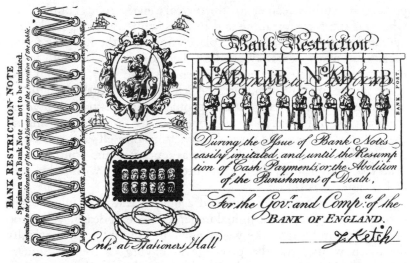

'Hanging' banknote used in protest against execution for forgery

was far from being the case. In 1767 Turlis received 5s for whipping Elizabeth Fletcher, Sarah Johnson and Anne Eaton, and a further 10s for whipping Abraham Johnson from the Mile End turnpike to London Hospital – a most suitable terminus. In the following century William Calcraft got £50 a year, but only 2s 6d per flogging he administered although he was paid an allowance for birches and whips. The low wages had to be made up by the many extras that went with the job. Surgeons paid for bodies to dissect, and rich victims handed over purses of gold to ensure a swift death. The deceased's clothing became the hangman's property, and the sale of the rope itself, cut into small sections, proved very lucrative.

Permitting the eager members of the public to touch the swinging corpse for luck or health was a good sideline. James Botting charged 2s 6d to allow those afflicted with wens to touch the corpse. Even the French swordsman from St Omer who executed Anne Boleyn received £23.6.8 as a fee, plus a new black suit and mask, together with a horned cap.

There were executioners operating outside London, of course, doing the same jobs – hanging, branding, flogging, burning witches and dismembering traitors – especially in the north of the country. Early in the last century John Curry held sway at York, as did his clients, whilst Thomas Young officiated in Glasgow until 1840.

The master of hempen ceremonies west of the Pennines was a Welshman called Old Ned, really named Edward Barlow, who pursued his ruthless career for thirty years, hated by the public, and who was the focus of abuse and missiles while on the scaffold. He operated mainly at Lancaster, a place known as 'the hanging town' because so many of its lawbreakers died longitudinally. No fewer than 276 felons were executed between 1782 and 1887, and Old Ned accounted for 131 of them. On 19 April 1817, with little thought for human suffering, he hanged nine people simultaneously, crowding them as close as jackets in a wardrobe in order to avoid re-stringing the gallows. He received several convictions himself, and was twice sentenced to transportation but he was reprieved and continued his grim task until he died about 1820, fittingly enough within the walls of Lancaster Castle.

Wigtown in Scotland once had a unique tradition whereby its executioner had to be a criminal under sentence of death. When too old to perform his tasks, he was hanged, but should he die naturally the town would lose the privilege of having its own hangman. However, Wigtown's 'Jock Ketch' fell ill and the townsfolk immediately assembled in order to hang him. Their evil intent was frustrated by his friends who, sitting him up in bed, surrounded him with the tools of his subsidiary trade, that of a cobbler. The townsfolk, satisfied that he had contracted a mere cold, left the man in peace. He promptly died, and Wigtown forfeited its right to have a hangman.

The ratepayers of Inverness may well have regretted ever having an executioner at all, for the fees and perquisites given to Donald Ross would have gladdened the heart of any council employee. He had a furnished house with free fuel, a delivery of oatmeal, and a fish from every basket brought to market. A penny was his for every sack of oatmeal sold in the market, and a peck of salt out of every cargo. Each year he was given a suit of clothes, two shirts, two pairs of stockings and shoes, and a hat. Christmas boxes also came his way, and he was paid £5 for each execution. No wonder the town council bitterly regretted the contract, for during his twenty years as hangman, Ross performed just three executions.

At long last the wind of change blew through the profession, bringing in its wake a new type of man, and a mercifully quicker death for the condemned. In 1874 William Marwood, then over fifty years of age, was appointed executioner and he introduced the scientifically assessed method of the 'long drop', which caused death instantly by dislocating the neck, rather than the previous slow strangulation. This took the victim's weight and other characteristics into consideration and the fall was adjusted accordingly, usually between five and eight feet. Too short a drop strangled; too long a drop decapitated – this latter actually occurring in 1885 when James Berry officiated at Norwich Castle.

Marwood, the master craftsman, brought a new dignity to the post of executioner. No one abused him or labelled him Jack Ketch, and the honest, conscientious man took pride in his methods. It was he who replaced the rough hempen slipknot with a metal ring which tightened the running noose instantly about the felon's throat, and the rapid descent did the rest in only seconds. The public's tolerance, if not respect, for the incumbent was not only due to Marwood's innovations. Crimes carrying the death penalty had been drastically reduced in number; hangings no longer took place in public, and society in general was becoming more educated, accepting that someone had to complete the processes of the nation's laws.

Just as Calcraft's signboard was displayed in Madame Tussaud's, so the public's interest in the new executioner required a wax facsimile of Marwood to be made. He posed frequently for the modellers accompanied by his pet dog, an old terrier, and meanwhile refreshing himself with gin and water, his favourite beverage. During his visits to the Chamber of Horrors in Madame Tussaud's he surveyed those he had hanged, their models soon to be joined by his own in a macabre tableau of execution. Marwood died of pneumonia in 1883, and was followed by the splendidly named Bartholomew Binns. Two years later James Berry took over and his waxen model also graced the Tussaud Museum.

The year 1892 saw James Billington in office, a position he held until 1906 when Henry Albert Pierrepoint became executioner. The Pierrepoints kept the noose in the family, so to speak, for Henry's brother Thomas succeeded him in 1924 and Henry's son Albert, after becoming an assistant in 1931, was chief hangman until his retirement in 1956.

These three dedicated and conscientious craftsmen officiated at over seven hundred executions during their fifty years or so in office. Albert carried out his arduous duty during World War II, despatching enemy spies and saboteurs. After the war, over two hundred war criminals, male and female, who had been condemned to death at the Nuremberg trials, met their end at his hands. Other executions followed, one being that of Ruth Ellis who, at 9am on 13 July 1955, was the last woman to be hanged in this country. After Albert's retirement the duties were carried out by Harry Allen and his deputies and thirty-four further executions took place before the death penalty was effectively abolished in 1964.

In the preceding chapters it will have been apparent that while both men and women were tortured and executed, those who actually turned the screw, wielded the whip, or adjusted the halter were always men. But for those who attended Irish hangings, especially in the town of Roscommon, things were very different.

In that town, early in the last century, executions took place outside the gaol, a tall building situated in the market place. A doorway pierced its third storey, over which projected a beam and pulley. Level with this entrance, or rather exit, was a hinged platform with a sliding bolt holding it horizontal until the noose had been positioned and prayers recited. When the bolt was withdrawn, the platform would drop with a terrifying crash against the prison wall, leaving the felon suspended from the beam.

Unusual as these gallows were, they attracted less attention than the executioner, for that official was no hulking brute or bearded bully, but a woman – a hangwoman! She was known as Lady Betty, and acted as Finisheress of the Law in the Connaught district for many years. Disdaining to wear a mask on the scaffold, for there was little point in disguising herself, she was described in the Dublin University Magazine of January 1850 as 'a middle aged, stout made, dark eyed, swarthy complexioned but by no means forbidding looking woman' and if her looks turned men on, her intentions were to turn them off, for she carried out frequent executions during those turbulent years of Irish history.

She was born in County Kerry, married young, and had a son, but such was her violent disposition that he left home to become a soldier. After much service abroad he returned asking for a night's lodgings, but he decided to keep his identity secret until he had ascertained whether his mother had mellowed at all. Far from mellowing, Lady Betty promptly murdered him for his money while he slept. She was arrested, tried, and sentenced to death along with a motley band of thieves, poachers and cattle rustlers. As no executioner was available, Lady Betty agreed to hang her fellow felons and, evidently enjoying the experience, she accepted the job on a permanent basis and became the official hangwoman for the district.

Not content with riding in the cart, adjusting the halter and operating the drop, she also performed the ancillary duty of gibbetting the cadavers afterwards. In minor cases, where the court merely imposed a flogging, Lady Betty wielded the whip with gusto, attracting large crowds along the route. Despite her dreadful crime and macabre choice of career, she was not uneducated and indeed took to sketching charcoal portraits of her victims on the walls of her room in Roscommon.

Her fame spread far and wide throughout Ireland during the 1820s and 1830s, and many were the disobedient children whose behaviour suddenly improved on hearing their parents threaten 'Huggath a' Pooka!' – Here's Lady Betty!

# 12 Humour on the Scaffold

*If I am to be the reason for jollity*
*The causing of crowds and a sense of frivolity*
*Then let us hasten – let no time be lost*
*That bonnets and hats in the air may be tossed.*
*For nothing can start – nothing can happen*
*Till I do appear and my poor neck be snappen.*

It says a lot for the human spirit that despite the fate that awaited them, many condemned men could summon up a witty comment or a wry remark, in their final hours. Ungenerously, it could be attributed to supping too deep of St Giles' Bowl, or sheer bravado inspired by the biggest audience they'd ever faced. Be that as it may, grudging tribute must be paid to such men, begrudged if only because we could not see ourselves acting similarly in the shadow of the gallows or within swinging range of the axe.

Wife murderer William Borwick, while standing on the scaffold of York's Tyburn, commented that he hoped the rope was strong enough, because if it broke he'd fall to the ground and be crippled for life! Another man, Patrick Clanachan, had been sentenced in 1709 'to be taken on 31 August, between the hours of 12 and 2 in the afternoon, to the gyppet at Wigtown and there to hang till he was dead.' Clanachan, who incidentally was the last man to be hanged at Wigtown, was being dragged along on a hurdle en route to the gallows and, observing spectators rushing past in order to get a good place in the square, called out 'Tak yer time, boys; there'll be no fun till I get there!'

The witticism of Donald, another Scotsman was reported in the *Courant* of 21 August 1828. Apparently, the choice of the tree on which he was to be hanged was left to the condemned man, and so Donald selected a young sapling. When the sheriff pointed out that the tree was much too small, Donald replied, 'Oich, but I'm in no hurry. I'll just wait till it grows!'

This humorous offer to delay things was similar to the comments made by Sir Walter Raleigh. After thirteen years imprisonment in the Tower of London, he was sentenced to die on 29 October 1618 at Westminster. On the morning of the fateful day, he had supped a cup of sack brought to him by his yeoman warder and, when asked whether he had enjoyed it, Raleigh said that he had, but that it would have been even better if he could have tarried over it! Later, on the scaffold, his old friend Sir Hugh Ceeston was prevented from joining him there. 'Prithee, never fear,' Raleigh commented, 'I shall have a place.' Feeling the edge of the axe he remarked: 'This is a sharp medicine, but it will cure all diseases.'

The sayings of those noblemen imprisoned in the Tower have survived longer than those of ordinary criminals. Bishop Latimer, suffering the bitter weather of 1553, complained to the Lieutenant of the Tower, Sir John Bridges, about his living conditions. 'For,' he said, 'they intend to burn me; but unless you give me some fuel in my cell, I shall die of cold.' Stowe relates an account of Sir Thomas More: 'when he was to lay his Head down on the Block, he having a great grey Beard, said to the Executioner, I pray you let me lay my Beard forward over the Block lest you should cut it; for though you have a Warrant to cut off my Head, you have none to cut my Beard.'

Two centuries later, on 9 April 1747, Tower Hill was a vast sea of faces, tens of thousands having gathered to see the old rebel Simon Lord Lovat beheaded. So packed were the crowds that some scaffolding collapsed, killing ten people instantly, and another ten died the next day, including the carpenter responsible for the construction work and his wife who had been selling liquor beneath it. When the eighty-year-old Lord Lovat was going up the steps on to the platform, assisted by his two yeoman warders, he looked around at the vast assembly. 'God save us', he exclaimed, 'why should there be such a commotion about taking off an old grey head that cannot get up a few steps without three bodies to support it?' To James Fraser his solicitor he commented, 'I am going to heaven; but you must continue to crawl a little longer in this evil world.'

Another prisoner from the Tower was Lord Strafford, who had been falsely accused of treason by Titus Oates. When he mounted the scaffold on 29 December 1681 he was loudly jeered at and abused by the rabble, and when he appealed to the officials present Sheriff Bethel brutally replied, 'Sir, we have orders to stop nobody's breath but yours.'

Humour as cynical as Bethel's was fortunately rare, but a similar instance had occurred previously when, in 1549, the Mayor of

Bodmin took part in an uprising. So minimal was his participation that he was confident of an acquittal, and this was further endorsed by the visit of Sir Anthony Kingston, who invited himself to dinner with the Mayor. The purpose of his visit, said Sir Anthony, was to hang a man, and so after the meal they adjourned to the newly constructed gallows. 'Think you it is strong enough?' queried his lordship 'It is indeed,' assured the Mayor, only to recoil as Sir Anthony retorted, 'Well then, get you up, it's for you' – and the mayor was hanged forthwith.

Tyburn also had its share of local wits. In the eighteenth century Dr Dodds, King's Chaplain, ran into debt, forged signatures and even

Lord Lovat beheaded for treason on Tower Hill

'descended so low as to become the editor of a newspaper'. Forgery carried the death penalty and, as the cart stopped beneath the tree, a very heavy shower of rain fell, with a further deluge as the Doctor put his blindfold on. One of the officials held an umbrella over the condemned man's head, prompting an observer to remark that it was quite unnecessary as the Doctor was going to a place where he might be dried.

On the same gallows, on 19 July 1694, a man named Paynes met his end for murdering half a dozen people. Before being turned off he 'kickt the Ordinary [prison chaplain] out of the cart and pulled his own shoes off, sayeing, hee'd contradict the old proverb, and not dye in them.'

This was a sentiment echoed by Richard Hayward at Newgate in 1760, and reported in the annual register. Taking off his jacket and shoes, he took others from his friend and donned those saying, 'Thus will I defeat my enemies; they have often said I should die in *my* coat and shoes, and I am determined to die in neither.' His fellow prisoners, watching from the cell windows, called out their regrets at his fate. 'I want none of your pity,' rejoined Hayward. 'Keep your snivelling till it be your own turn.' Then, turning to the crowd, he called for three cheers, giving the introductory 'hip hip' himself as the noose was positioned about his neck. He was turned off before the last cheer had died away.

Condemned prisoners were always the focus of public attention, not only for their sayings but also for their choice of clothes. Mrs Anne Turner, guilty of hideously poisoning Sir Thomas Overbury in the Bloody Tower in 1613, was instructed by the judge to wear a yellow starched cobweb-lawn ruff; this being a fashion she had introduced in the royal court. She duly obeyed, only to find that the hangman also wore a large ruff made of yellow paper with matching cuffs. Yellow starch immediately went out of fashion.

Another material followed suit, as it were, over two centuries later when, on 13 November 1847, Frederick and Maria Manning were hanged for murder by executioner Calcraft. Maria chose black satin for her execution, and it too instantly lost favour with the public.

As mentioned earlier, the chaplain accompanying the prisoners faced many hazards, but none so dire as that reported in the *Derby Mercury* of 6 April 1738:

last month Will Summers and John Tipping were executed here for housebreaking. At the gallows, the hangman was intoxicated with liquor and, believing that there were three for execution, attempted to put one of the ropes round the parson's neck as he stood in the cart, and was with much difficulty prevented by the gaoler from doing so.

Warders too always ran the risk of revenge by prisoners. In 1726 a prisoner called Burnworth had murdered a workman in the Mint and was condemned to death. Before the execution procession got under way, he threatened his warder that if his body wasn't decently buried after hanging, he'd meet him in a dark alleyway and pull his nose off!

Even in more recent times, humour of a sort was never far away. In

1817 executioner James Botting ignored the jeers and insults hurled at him by a gang of hooligans near his home and, when asked why he didn't retaliate, James commented drily, 'I never quarrel with the customers.' Oddly enough, one of the group ran foul of the law and was actually hanged by Botting later that year.

Double murderer James Rush was executed on 21 April 1894; quite a gourmet, he selected 'roast pig with plenty of plum sauce' for his last meal, and dined well. Next morning on the scaffold he advised the hangman to position the noose a little higher. 'Don't hurry', he said patiently, 'take your time!'

A violent scene occurred in court in May 1896 when Albert Milsom and Henry Fowler accused each other of the murder of their victim. Both were found guilty but they still fought, and on the scaffold they were kept apart by having another man, John Seaman, positioned between them. It is reported that Seaman's last words were 'It's the first time in my life I've ever been a bloody peacemaker!'

Punishment places other than the scaffold also provoked humorous comments. The pillory was often known as 'the stretchneck', and this was never more true than when one such device became so weatherbeaten that the footboard collapsed, causing the culprit to hang by neck and wrists. When released he took legal action, sued the council for negligence, and won his case.

Another pillory, erected in the market place in Manchester, was mounted on a tall pole. Being round in shape, it was promptly christened 'the tea-table'. One unfortunate occupant of the device explained sarcastically to an enquirer that he wasn't being pilloried but was 'celebrating his nuptials with Miss Wood,' and a friend who was being flogged by the beadle was in reality dancing at the wedding. The pillory was also the punishment awarded to William Duffin and Thomas Lloyd who, not content with escaping from Fleet prison in London, actually delayed their departure in order to nail a notice to its gates advertising, 'This prison to let, and peaceable possession will be given by the present tenants on or before 1 January 1793.'

Doubtless the crowds attending their eventual punishment were duly sympathetic, and sometimes this sentiment even affected some of the officials present. On one occasion, at Olney in Buckinghamshire, in 1783, a man was accused of stealing ironwork during a fire in the town, and was sentenced to be whipped at the cart's tail. As he was being secured there, he pretended to resist strongly, and the charade was continued by the beadle who wielded the whip with his right hand, pulling the thongs through his left hand between strokes. The 'blood' that drenched the culprit's shoulders, however, was the red ochre previously smeared in the beadle's left palm!

The constable, present to ensure the correct number of lashes and the severity of the punishment realised the subterfuge and, in order to stop the pretence, promptly set about the beadle with his cane of office. At this point a young lady burst forth from the crowd and, to defend the beadle, belaboured the constable about the head and shoulders. And so, as described by the poet William Cowper, at that time lay preacher at Olney, 'the spectacle was such that I could not forbear to relate how the beadle thrashed the thief, the constable the beadle, and the lady the constable, and how the thief was the only person who suffered nothing!'

Finally, a hanging with a happy ending. Margaret Dixon, a fisherman's wife, had an illegitimate child and was accused later of putting it to death. She was executed at Edinburgh on 19 June 1728 and, after hanging for an hour, her body was cut down. The funeral cortege set off for her native village Musselburgh, about five miles away. As it was a hot day, the sad procession made frequent stops for refreshment, and it was while halted at the inn at Pepper-Mill that the mourners received the shock of their lives. As they sat quenching their thirst by the open cart which bore the coffin, a gasp of horror came from one of them and all eyes focussed on the coffin lid as it slowly slipped to one side.

Some of the attendants fled in terror but others, more courageous, approached the coffin – whereupon the 'deceased' Margaret sat up. In the commotion, a guest of the inn-keeper had the presence of mind to open one of her veins, a universal cure in those days, and after nursing and care she revived sufficiently to be able to walk the next day. Under Scottish law, she had been executed and so no further action could be taken against her. Legally she had ceased to exist, a fact that mattered little in an age without national insurance, income tax, passports and other twentieth-century essentials. Her marriage too had also ceased to be valid but the 'widower' sought her out, reconciliation followed and a few days after being hanged Margaret remarried her husband with the church packed to the doors. No ill effects followed her awful experience, and she lived for a further twenty-five years, dying in 1753.

# For the Record

1076 First execution by the axe, Earl of Huntingdon.

1208 First witchcraft trial, Gideon, a sorcerer, acquitted.

1241 First person hanged, drawn and quartered in England; William Marise, pirate.

1250 Abolition of trial by fire or water.

23.8.1305 First recorded head displayed on London Bridge; Sir William Wallace, Scottish patriot.

1450 First recorded use of the Tower of London rack.

1547 Abolition of boiling to death.

1612 Last burning alive in England, for heresy, Edward Wightman at Lichfield, Staffs.

1636 Abolition of branding 'S' for slave.

21.5.1640 Last recorded use of Tower rack, John Archer, rioter.

1648 Abolition of burning for heresy, in England.

29.7.1649 Greatest number hanged at one time at Tyburn, London, 23 men, 1 woman.

30.4.1650 Last men executed by Halifax Gibbet, John Wilkinson and Anthony Mitchell, thieves.

1685 Last man executed by Scottish Maiden, 9th Earl of Argyll.

1686 Last hanging for witchcraft, Alice Molland.

1690 Last recorded torture in Scotland.

1697 Last burning alive for heresy in Scotland.

1708 Abolition of torture in Scotland.

1712 Last trial for witchcraft in England, Jane Wenham, reprieved.

1722 Last witch believed to be burned in Scotland.

1740 Last reported *peine forte et dure* (pressing) in Ireland.

9.4.1747 Last man executed by the axe, Simon Lord Lovat, Jacobite rebel.

5.5.1760 First use of trapdoor in hanging (the drop), Earl Ferrers, murderer.

6.1780 Last executions on Tower Hill, William M'Donald, Charlotte Gardener, Mary Roberts, rioters.

7.11.1783 Last execution at Tyburn, John Austin, robber.

9.12.1783 First executions at Newgate Prison (ten persons).

1786 Last public execution at Newgate by burning (woman, hanged first).

1789 Last woman burned in England, Christian Murphy, alias Christian Bowman, coiner.

5.6.1790 Abolition of burning of women who murdered their husbands.

1791 Abolition of death penalty for witchcraft.

1791 Abolition of whipping of female vagrants.

1809 Last recorded ducking of scolds, Jenny Pipes née Jane Corran.

1814 Abolition of beheading.

1817 Last person sentenced to suffer ducking stool, Sarah Leeke, but pool too shallow!

1820 Abolition of whipping of women.

1.5.1820 Last men beheaded by the axe (after death), Cato Street Conspirators.

1827 Abolition of *peine dure et forte*.

31.12.1829 Last man hanged for forgery, Thomas Maynard.

1832 Abolition of hanging for cattle, horse and sheep stealing.

1832 Abolition of dissection after hanging.

22.6.1832 Last person to suffer the pillory, Peter James Bossy.

11.8.1832 Last man gibbetted in England (hanged in chains after death), James Cook, murderer.

1833 Abolition of hanging for house breaking.

25.7.1834 Abolition of gibbetting.

1837 Abolition of the pillory.

1861 Last execution for attempted murder, Martin Doyle.

9.7.1864 First murder on a train, Franz Müller (executed).

28.7.1865 Last public hanging in Scotland, Dr Edward William Pritchard.

26.5.1868 Last public hanging in England, Michael Barrett, Fenian murderer.

13.8.1868 First non-public hanging in England, Thomas Wells, murderer, Maidstone Prison, Kent.

1870 Abolition of hanging, drawing, quartering penalty.

11.6.1872 Last person to suffer in the stocks, Mark Tuck, drunk and disorderly.

1879 Abolition of branding.

9.6.1896  Last triple hanging at Newgate Prison.

1906  Abolition of hanging of persons under age of sixteen.

1932  Abolition of hanging of persons under age of eighteen.

1955  Last woman executed in the United Kingdom, Ruth Ellis, murderess.

13.8.1964  Last executions in the United Kingdom, Peter Allen and Gwynne Owen, murderers.

# Select Bibliography

Abbott, G. *The Beefeaters of the Tower of London* (David & Charles, 1985)
Andrews, William. *Old Time Punishments* (William Andrews, 1890)
Bayley, J. *History of the Tower* (Jennings and Chaplin, 1830)
Bell, D. C. *Chapel in the Tower* (John Murray, 1877)
British Library. *Calendar of State Papers* (Domestic Series)
Carment. *Glimpses of the Olden Times* (1893)
Davey. *Tower of London* (1910)
*Dictionary of National Biography* (Oxford University Press)
Fox, C. *General Williamson's Diary* (Camden Society, 1912)
*Foxe's Book of Martyrs* (1563)
*Gentleman's Magazine* (1750, 1829)
*Gregory's Chronicles* (Camden Society, 1876)
*Hall's Chronicles* (ed 1809)
*Holinshed's Chronicles* (1586)
Jackson. *Newgate Calendar* (1818)
*John Evelyn's Diary* (ed 1850)
*Machyn's Diary of a London Resident* (Camden Society, 1848)
Marks. *Tyburn Tree* (Brown, Langham & Co, 1910)
*Notable British Trials* series
*Notes and Queries* (1851)
Parry, Sir Edward. *The Bloody Assize* (1929)
*Stowe's Annals* (1580, 1615)
Sutherland Gower, Lord. *Tower of London* (1902)
Thornbury, Walter. *Old & New London* (Cassell, Petter & Galpin, 1873)
Timbs. *Romance of London* (Warne & Co, 1865)
Tower of London Records

# Acknowledgements

To the Resident Governor, and the Master of the Armouries, Her Majesty's Tower of London. Also to the staffs of the British Library, London, Lancaster Library and Calderdale Libraries, Halifax, Yorkshire.